Leaving the Convent

For Ste. Thérèse of Lisieux

Ex-Nuns

Women Who Have Left the Convent

by Gerelyn Hollingsworth

McFarland & Company, Inc., Publishers
Jefferson, North Carolina, and London

Library of Congress Cataloging in Publication Data

Hollingsworth, Gerelyn.
Ex-nuns : women who have left the convent.

Bibliography: p.
Includes index.
1. Ex-nuns—United States. I. Title.
BX4668.2.H64 1985   305′.9222   84-43207

ISBN 0-89950-156-7 (alk. paper)

Printed in the United States of America.

McFarland   Box 611   Jefferson NC 28640

Table of Contents

Preface

In 1966 there were more than 180,000 nuns in American convents. By 1985 fewer than 120,000 remained. In nineteen years, sixty thousand women left the convent.

What happened in the religious communities to make one third of their members depart? Why had so many women entered convents in the first place? What did they expect to find? How did the realities of community life differ from their expectations? How did the stress of leaving the convent affect their physical and spiritual health? Why did the communities treat their departing members with so little justice? Why has the official church ignored the exodus, and extended no healing hand to the sixty thousand?

The women continuing in religious life are aging, and few candidates are entering convents: the communities will not survive the century. Was their collapse inevitable? Their chronicles contain accounts of the lives of bold and unusual women: they reveal as well the development of those aspects of convent life which have brought it to its present terminal condition.

How do nuns of today regard their former sisters? How do they explain the departure of so many? What future do they see for women's communities? Has the hierarchy noticed the empty motherhouse? Will Catholics be offered an explanation?

I had many questions for nuns and ex-nuns. They answered with candor and generosity in face-to-face interviews, in telephone conversations, and in written responses to a questionnaire. Their answers make up Part One of this book. Part Two is an examination of the American communities.

vii

As agriculture replaced gathering and hunting, there were women who chose not to settle down, but preferred to continue with the old ways and remain free. These unattached—loose—women survived in Europe down the centuries, but as Christianity replaced the pagan religions, such women came to be regarded with hostility. The earliest convents provided a refuge for women for whom camp following—one alternative for loose women—was distasteful. Nuns, like widows and matrons who served the people in active ministries, were free to resign without censure.

As the centuries passed and the church grew more powerful, widows and matrons were forbidden public ministry, and consecrated virgins were given rules written by men: it became difficult to leave a convent. Social custom allowed families to put unwanted daughters into religious life; women who were illegitimate or deformed or feeble-minded replaced the adventurous or scholarly or spiritual nuns of earlier days. Families could save money by putting daughters into convents; the dowry for a religious house was less than that for a bridegroom. Families would not want such daughters returning home to demand a share of an estate or to be troublesome in other ways. The church cooperated: solemn vows were instituted. To leave a convent was to go forth into apostasy; an ex-nun could not receive the sacraments, contract a valid marriage, or own property. Solemn vows, mentioned by Gratian, the founder of Canon law, in the 12th century, were defined by Boniface VIII in the 13th century. Ex-nuns came to be regarded with horror. Likewise women (called witches), camp followers (called whores), devotees of shrines, and other loose women of medieval Europe, they had to exist on the fringes of society. They were vulnerable and despised.

In the 16th century, Pius V further tightened solemn vows. Like his friend, St. Charles Borromeo, the pope doubted women's ability to go about responsibly. Nuns were more strictly enclosed than ever. Solemn vows, cloister, community life, and religious habits were imposed even on groups of women such as the Ursulines and the Visitandines who had banded together to instruct women and girls.

In the 18th century, Benedict XIV gave legitimate existence to religious congregations without solemn vows or enclosure, but not until the 20th century would active sisters be considered true religious; they lacked the solemn vows necessary for that designation.

With few exceptions, American sisters profess simple vows. From a juridical standpoint, leaving the convent is easy. Why then, on a social readjustment scale, is leaving a religious community ranked as a life change more stressful than a death in the family and as a predictor of illness more ominous than that after the loss of a spouse?

Part One: The Women

I. Why Did You Want to Become a Religious Sister?

My early life was a series of catastrophes, but without all the troubles I might never have turned to religion. As it was, I felt an intimacy with God from about age nine. From then on I always intended to enter religious life. My father died when I was six, leaving three children. My mother was in and out of mental hospitals. I had a strong inclination toward the contemplative life. I was devoted to Therese of Lisieux, and dreamed of living a life of prayer, silence, and needlework. I applied to a contemplative convent, but when they heard my mother was mentally ill, their cordiality sort of dried up. This left me choosing my grade school teachers' community. I didn't really want to be a teacher, but somehow my focus was on religious life per se, and therefore the type of work the sisters did wouldn't make much difference. How little I knew. I longed from the beginning to merge my life with other people who were as earnest as I was about seeking God and living with him. This was really what I thought religious life would be, and the details didn't seem important. In 1954 I said goodbye to everything I had known, and took the train to the convent. I was in a daze. I was stepping off the world, but I knew I had to do it.

I wanted to do something worthwhile with my life. I wanted to serve God and other people. I entered in

1

1960 when I was seventeen. My father was an alcoholic. My mother's drinking killed her a year ago. My father lost his job my senior year, and I had to get away from home to find some peace and quiet. Marriage was out. I had a lousy image of married life from observing my parents, and boys only seemed to want to use me sexually. I wanted to be a Carmelite. I read the life of Therese of Lisieux, and began visiting a Carmelite monastery. My high school teachers found out. One of them suggested I see a priest she knew. He was one of the most Christlike people I have ever met. My teachers and the priest convinced me to enter my teachers' order. They said if it didn't work out, I could always enter Carmel, but if I went to Carmel first, I would never be able to enter their order.

I used to pray a lot. I went for long walks in the woods to talk with God. At fourteen, I got angry with God, and told him to get out of my life. I told him I hated him, and wanted him to leave me alone. I had an immediate guilt experience, and walked into town to see the parish priest for confession. He was not sensitive to my crisis of faith, so I left the church. Two years later, I joined the Baptist church and was involved with them until college. In college I was in a Baptist group that was involved with the anti-war movement. I hung out in a coffee house, and eventually got involved with a group of charismatics. I had a falling out with my parents because of my anti-war stance, and had to leave school. I began praying at a monastery. I felt called. I felt God wanted me to live a vowed life. I met some teaching sisters. Their vocation team recruited me. I entered in August, 1974.

I wanted to be a nun from first grade on. We were taught that it was the highest vocation. The order I entered had its motherhouse in our home town. In the evening

I would sit on my back steps and look at the beautiful convent, and dream of being a nun. I entered in 1945. My father had remarried, and I could not get along with my stepmother. The sooner I could get away from home, the better. Also, it was the only way I would get to college. That's what I thought then.

I entered the convent in 1951 when I was sixteen. I thought I could run away from life, but I developed a stomach ulcer in the first year. I had planned to enter the convent for years. My mother encouraged me in this. My older sister was in the convent. I wanted a totally cloistered order, but didn't have the knowledge or energy to pursue this. I was one of eleven children. We had to help with the younger children. I missed seeing the Wizard of Oz because it was my turn for babysitting. All my brothers entered the seminary.

I first thought about entering the convent at twelve or thirteen. I went to public school, but was very impressed with the sisters who taught us religion after school. I was attracted to the mysteries I felt they represented. I entered in 1962, age twenty-two.

I entered in 1942 at twenty. I wanted to enter after senior year, but my father insisted I finish college first. I was so concerned with entering the convent, that I failed to enjoy my college years.

I read a book on leprosy. This helped me focus on the way in which I could serve God, something I had intended to do since first grade. I discussed my vocation with a priest. "Go to the lepers," he said. I entered the convent in 1929. I was sixteen. My father took me to the mother-house where we had a visit of less than a half-hour before he was dismissed.

I entered in 1948. I had wanted to be a nun as long as I could remember. I read lives of saints and mission booklets, and sometimes dressed up as a religious. I wanted to enter Maryknoll, but they wanted college girls. I didn't want to wait that long. I was extremely shy. Both my parents were very religious.

I was twenty-one when I entered the convent. It was 1955. I was serious, shy, and had a strong desire to do good. I also wanted further education.

I guess I'll never know why I entered the convent. My dad was domineering and gave me an Electra complex. I wanted to be like my older sister, a nun, who was his favorite child. I was afraid to go to college and compete, because I was upper class and very ugly. I thought God really wanted me to help people by being a teacher. I entered in 1958. For the first time I got the spotlight away from my older sister. I was seventeen.

In my junior year in college I went to a mission with a Catholic friend. I experienced such a piercing sense of Utter Reality, that I lost my belief in Unbelief. I joined the Catholic Church. After five years of seeking, I entered the convent. It was 1938.

I was almost eighteen when I entered in 1960. I was unable to set a goal for myself for after high school. I was afraid. My upbringing in an authoritatian home, my life in the Catholic ghetto, and my education in Catholic schools made me fear the evil world beyond the borders of Catholicism. I had noticed the recognition the girls got who entered the convent. I needed recognition, and I needed to make my father proud. I also needed to devote my life to a social cause, affiliated with the church.

My mother died when I was six, and my dad remarried within a year. My stepmother found it difficult to inherit three small children. My childhood was miserable. My stepmother was a perfectionist as was my dad. I never felt loved or wanted. They were extremely strict, and totally unaffectionate toward my sisters or me. They doted on their own son. I used all my energy to try to please them and prove that I was worthwhile. I did well in school, and everyone thought well of me except my parents. I was never permitted to make decisions by myself. If I did, they were wrong. I thought about the convent off and on throughout grade school and high school. I entered after senior year. I was afraid God might want me to be a nun, and I wouldn't be happy if I didn't do what God wanted. Also, my life had been totally useless to that point, and I wanted to do something worthwhile. I used to pray every night that I'd live to go to the convent. I was eighteen when I entered in 1963.

I was born in 1939 to an intact Catholic family. My mother was a daily communicant. We said the family rosary daily. My parents were very moral. I was the youngest of four. My older sister entered the convent when I was in first grade. I entered in 1957, aged eighteen. I entered the same order my sister had. They had been my teachers. I probably entered the convent because I saw my older sister get a great deal of attention.

———————

I was a musically talented child. My parents were musicians. They pushed me to be disciplined in a way that drove me to rebel. By the time I was a teenager, I was overweight and sullen, achieving only half of what I could in school, and feeling guilty for even being alive. I was attracted to the church because there I was accepted for whatever I was. I felt one night a pressure to make a decision regarding this, and I came to the conclusion that I had a vocation. I resolved then and there to be a nun. I felt immense relief that I would not have to deal with the problems of living in the world. I had convinced myself that I was not cut out for that anyway. I chose the order which showed the most interest in me and my talents. I entered in 1964 at the age of eighteen. I considered going to college first, but a sister was sent to convince me otherwise.

———————

I wanted to be a religious in order to serve God. I grew up in a religious family. My father died in an auto accident when I was two. My mother raised seven children alone. I was quite introverted, shy and malleable. I can never remember wanting to be anything but a sister my entire life. I entered in 1972, aged twenty.

———————

My desire to become a religious sister was simply to live my life for God. I came from an Irish Catholic family of nine children. I am second to the oldest. I was the oldest girl. After high school I worked for a year for an insurance company. I see myself as a quiet, serious person with a strong competitive drive held back by an inferiority complex. This is not the image I project to others. They see me as fully in control. I was about fourteen when I began thinking about entering the convent. I had two desires when entering, to have a strong vow of poverty and to do social work. Since the orders that did social work carried a small amount of cash with them, I decided to enter a teaching order which was semi-cloistered and had a strict vow of poverty. I entered when I was eighteen. The year was 1954.

The thought of religious life was prominent from early days, but so were the ideas of being an actress, a writer, etc. I wanted to be a missionary sister because of my adventurous spirit. Also, the convent seemed one sure way of getting away from a dull, sometimes unhappy life. My parents came to this country at the turn of the century from Ireland. My mother worked as a housemaid. She sent much of her earnings home to Ireland. My father was self-educated, but lacking academic degrees or a specialty, he had to work as a laborer. This was hard for him. He became an alcoholic. He was never abusive, but I was embarrassed when I saw him drunk on the street. I learned to love music, McCormick's golden voice. Once we had a gorgeous piano, but instead of letting me take lessons, my mother gave it to the nuns. I resented this. I was too serious as a child. I was the oldest of six. My mother placed a great deal of responsibility on me. I was unhappy and not greatly loved. I entered the convent in 1931. I was fourteen.

I was too much like my mom for her to appreciate me. I was considered a problem child. I thought I was a pretty good kid. My friend's parents praised me. You might say I was a Dr. Jekyll and Mr. Hyde type of person.

I did not tell my parents I was going to enter the convent until they pressed me to apply to college. I was working at a camp run by a group of missionary sisters. When they realized my interest, they encouraged me, and made me feel welcome in their presence. They allowed me to accompany them in visiting the sick, the poor, illegal aliens, and persons wanting instruction in the faith. I entered in 1966 at age eighteen.

I always wanted religious life. I was the oldest of four. My father died when I was eight. I went to college full time freshman year, but then, for financial reasons, had to switch to evening classes. For three years I worked for the telephone company. I entered the convent in 1964. I was twenty two.

I entered in 1950 at the age of fourteen. I cannot remember a time since first grade that I did not want to become a nun. Nuns were my role models, both as teachers and as religious women. As a child, I never made a distinction between the two. I wanted to attain the highest vocation for a woman, and I wanted to teach. My vocation was as simple and straightforward as that. My parents were pious, Catholic, petit bourgeois, French Canadians. I was the oldest of eight, but never felt burdened by responsibility. My parents encouraged my intellectual bent, and were proud of the hours I spent in the public libraries. I lived in a warm, supportive, and very Catholic family environment. I was very independent-minded. I could do whatever I wanted, even leave home at fourteen.

My mother was outwardly nice, but deeply rejecting. My father was an alcoholic. I learned that I could get approval by excelling in school, and being active in the parish. I joined the convent to help heal people. I also got out of a hell of a home life. I entered in 1974, age twenty.

I decided to enter the convent in sixth grade. Religion was very meaningful that year. I found prayer a personal experience with a living God. I lost the sense of God's presence in seventh and eighth grade, but I decided to go to the convent to find it again. I entered after eighth grade. I was fourteen. It was 1962.

I entered the convent in 1959 at the age of 17. I knew I would not be happy married to the kind of boy my parents could afford. Our house was squalid. I was adopted, and my parents disliked me. I wanted to prove that I was good, and I wanted more education. My parents wanted me to go to work after high school, at an insurance company.

I had a very unhappy home life that I wanted to escape from. We were upper-class, well-educated, sophisticated. I was the oldest of four. My parents' drinking, psychological abuse, and physical and emotional neglect caused me confusion and guilt. I entered the convent because I didn't realize there were other options open to me. No one said, "You can go to college," or "You can study music." I was drawn to the nuns. I needed privacy. I needed to be alone and silent. I am contemplative by nature. My father died when I was a child. My sister and I were not allowed to attend the funeral. I stood at a window of our house day after day when the sun was in the right position for my father to come home. He didn't come. I spent my years from four to nine

waiting and watching for my father. Sometimes I would
see a man who looked like my father. I would run up
to him and take his hand. My mother remarried. My
stepfather was a Catholic, and sent us to Catholic school.
We were baptized all at once. I entered the convent
in 1955. I was seventeen.

A priest told me that if I thought about becoming a
nun, it was God who placed the thought there. If I didn't
follow the idea of a religious vocation, I would have
to answer to God at the end of my life. My family in-
formed me that I was on my own. They moved to a
town about three hours away, and left me in a town
I barely knew with an elderly woman who was looking
for a boarder. I entered the convent in 1953. I was
eighteen years old.

I was part of a Pied Piper wave. A nun at my high school
was the Pied Piper, and my friends and I were the mice.
We all had crushes on her and on another nun. They
invited us to visit them at the motherhouse. The beauty
and tranquility of the motherhouse attracted me. The
nuns seemed like saints. All my best friends were going.
I didn't want to be left out. I entered in 1958 when I
was eighteen.

I was the oldest of three children. My parents were
Hispanic, and bilingual. I guess my greatest sorrow
as a child was the fact that my parents separated when
I was eleven. In my senior year in high school, I made
a retreat during which the priest spoke about religious
life. I felt the words were directed at me. It was a very
emotional but scary moment. I knew my parents would
object strongly. Hispanic people do not mind if a man

becomes a priest; there is a sort of status about this vocation, but a girl is born to be a wife and mother. I broke their hearts when I entered, but I felt the call with such urgency, and was so in love with the person of Christ that nothing else mattered. I am outgoing, gregarious, impulsive, compulsive, and independent. This latter quality made dealing with authority very difficult. I entered in 1942. I was twenty.

II. Please Describe Your Postulancy and Novitiate.

I remember the postulancy as a fairly happy time. We went to classes at the college on the motherhouse grounds. We attended class with the "lay" students, but we were a group apart, and were not to socialize beyond bare politeness. We wore mid-calf black dresses, black stockings, and nun's shoes. To pay for our education, we washed dishes after meals in the college dining rooms, and cleaned the motherhouse and college buildings. I loved it. Now, of course, they don't have enough postulants to undertake such tasks, and they think it is demeaning, but I loved it. Apart from manual labor and studying, we had times in chapel and spiritual reading. This spiritual reading was an example of the guidance we were given. The superior would read from an insipid book such as **Keys to the Third Floor.** We would listen and darn stockings. There was no force in the community to form us, just one book after another. In the summer, when the entire community was present, Father Somebody or Other would come and preach a retreat. Then everybody would be on a new bandwagon. At one point it was the letters of our founder, an eighteenth-century priest, cold, forbidding, nail-yourself-to-the-cross. In the novitiate we had no college classes, just one theology class. The novice mistress regretted letting us take this course because we argued all during recreation about social justice. She trained us in matters of form: how to walk like a nun, talk like a nun, eat like a nun, how not to be real, spontaneous, human. This sounds more bitter than I really feel. Now I feel pity. So much potential and good will came in, and so little came of it.

We took college courses in the postulancy. We were asked to choose what we wanted to study. I chose journalism first, law second, and psychology third. Our order's college offered none of these, so I was assigned to study English with education as a minor. There was an abundance of food. There was always a snack following afternoon recreation. I gained ten pounds my first year. Eating was a favorite pastime. I loved the silence, the woods and hills, the discipline.

During my two initiate years, I lived in a parish convent with fourteen professed sisters. I worked at an outside job, but took part in all community activities. I had instructions once a week with my director, a member of the formation team. Instructions consisted of readings such as "Why Am I Afraid To Tell You Who I Am." A priest taught us a class on "The Human Adventure." Even though the formation team kept an eye on us, we were pretty much on our own. Sometimes a particular event was "highly recommended," but nobody could force us to participate. The four members of my class entered novitiate in 1976. We wrote our own ceremony. We purchased green T-shirts, and had the word NOVICE printed on the front so the old sisters could tell who we were. My class had quite a struggle with the formation team. The team decided we could use some therapy. We found out they were using the therapist to find out things about us. We decided to confront the team. We found out that even though they talked about "choice," they really meant, "do what we say or get out."

We had to do cleaning and laundry. The postulants and novices had always done this work. In the old days there were more of them, but the community expected the same amount of work from us, even though we were few in number. The whole formation process was on an experimental basis while I was in. Four of the seven novices were in therapy.

———————

I loved the postulancy and novitiate: lots of study, regular meals, manual labor. Most of all I loved studying. The novice mistress was hard as nails, but that was an inspiration. The problem was, she had never taught school. She trained us to be contemplatives, although we were to spend our lives in the classroom.

———————

Why wasn't someone observant enough to see I didn't belong? We studied the rule, Latin, logic and ethics. I knew how to sew, so I was assigned to the sewing room. My novice mistress made a promise which I am seeing fulfilled now. My convent years prepared me for now!

———————

I felt a real lack of being in touch with the outside world. We were not allowed to read newspapers. Schooling stopped except for classes in the liturgy and scripture. The order of the day became very boring. I felt cut off from my family. Recreation was almost nonexistent except for a little volleyball and swimming in the summer. I didn't like being separated from the community. I didn't like being treated as a child. I did like the silence.

———————

In the postulancy the food was good, even though the

war was still on. I was hardly aware that the outside
world was struggling. Recreation was childish games.
Training in religious matters was at a minimum. In
the novitiate we were required to do some demanding
physical work, extensive cleaning, kitchen work and
garden work such as picking fruit. We had daily classes
on the office and the history of the order, and I had
a correspondence course in education. I liked the novitiate
because of the freedom from outside pressure. I disliked
being isolated from the professed sisters.

————————

We spent our time washing dishes, washing and waxing
floors, and cleaning bathrooms. The only schooling we
had was on the Catechism of the Vows. For recreation
we darned stockings. We were given sulphur and molasses
in the refectory; whatever was placed before us we
were required to eat or drink. Sometimes they gave
us a "good dose of epsom salts." I liked the novice mistress
and my companions, and wondered when we were going
to learn to meditate and pray. No preparation was given
for the community's work. We weren't trained for anything, spiritual life or profession. We heard about two
things, blind obedience and keeping the rule. As a sixteen
year old who trusted God, I went along with everything.
I liked getting up early, breaking the ice in my basin,
washing up, going to chapel. I liked the silence.

————————

I disliked the novice mistress intensely. I told myself
if I could live with her for two and a half years, I would
be a saint. She was the mistress, the boss, the king,
queen, and jack. We were young, tender, ignorant, and
full of good will. The novice mistress told us to report
to her any failings of others. I could never rat on anyone.
I closed up into myself, and hated silently.

————————

I belonged to a teaching order, and our postulancy and
novitiate were devoted to getting teaching credentials.
We did housework three times a day. The food was plentiful. I gained fifty pounds during my postulancy. I was
sent to a psychologist because I couldn't decide if I
wanted to make vows or not. Recreation consisted of
walking, always in threes, gardening, card playing, square
dancing. Relationships were always distant. I liked
my postulancy mistress because she was interested
in each one of us, forty in all. I hated the novitiate,
the chapter of faults, table penances, having my head
shaved, kissing the floor.

I liked the camaraderie of the postulancy. The postulant
mistress was a warm and understanding woman. We
took college classes. The novitiate was another story.
We had only spiritual classes, and spent most of our
time in the laundry, at cleaning duties, and in the infirmary with the sick and retired sisters. I feared the
mistress of novices. She was large and domineering,
and liked the power she had over all the novices. It
was a confining year.

Food was plentiful and fattening. Our novice mistress
was always saying that a good appetite was the sign
of a vocation. I put on forty pounds in the postulancy.
We were trained in religious matters during our canonical
year. Our novice mistress was a Thomistic scholar,
and her classes were excellent. I liked the lack of responsibility and the structure.

I had mixed emotions as a postulant. I was excited about
my new life of mystery and romance, and I yearned
to know more about the spiritual life. But I was given

little attention and no praise, and I hated the menial work. We had classes taught by priests and professed nuns in church history, theology, religious life, and scripture. The food was delicious. I gained weight because I ate everything that was put before me. Relationships with others were not my strong point. I felt committed to what I was doing, and was willing to put up with parts of the life which were not palatable.

———————

I entered during the transition period. I was financially responsible for all medical, room and board, and schooling. I had finished two years of college. I finished up at the order's college. I majored in sociology and psychology. That was my choice. I got on well with the other novices. We had some recreation, but it was generally a mandatory group activity. I slept very little, and walked the halls until two or three every morning.

———————

My postulancy and novitiate were uneventful. Our time was spent praying and studying the history of the order. The food was excellent, and medical care was provided. Recreation was at designated times. My relationship with my superiors was one of deep respect on my part. Everyone was treated equally. I had a healthy relationship with my companions, and enjoyed their company. We received no preparation for the work we would do later. It was all about becoming a good religious. I enjoyed the peace and quiet.

———————

I was a postulant for a year. No effort was made to have me finish high school, even though the community had an academy on the motherhouse grounds. In fact, because they needed teachers, I was sent on mission. Although the nuns on the mission were kind, I was beginning to feel an air of unreality which would pursue me down the years. I should have left two years after I entered, but I was afraid to seek counsel. I wanted to be good, and good sisters did not express doubts. There was constant criticism. Minutiae and Victorian manners were important. We were not supposed to be intelligent or clever. We were not supposed to be attractive or singular in any way, just good little peas in a pod.

Putting it mildly, I was not at all prepared for what I found. We were allowed to talk only to each other or to the directress. Conversation was to be about the daily homily or the spiritual reading. We had no access to newspapers, magazines, or television. Our mail was read. I felt we were expected to return to childhood. We had to ask permission for everything. I got along well with Mother Mistress. Woe to those who did not. We had a class every day in which she announced changes in the cleaning schedule. We prayed six hours a day. It was a time of change. One week after I received the habit, we changed to experimental garb.

As a postulant, I had a close relationship with our mistress. As the time for receiving the habit drew near, I began to suffer fears and doubts. I couldn't sleep at night. I spent hours with our mistress discussing these things. The novitiate turned out to be a much better experience than I thought it would. I wondered about one thing. We were taught that celibacy was to free us to serve God's people, but we were never with them. When we passed a secular, it was with eyes downcast.

Our early training was basically negative with heavy emphasis on faults and failings. We had public confession of faults and public accusation by peers. There was an infinite amount of emphasis on avoiding particular friendships. The novitiate was a wonderful time of spiritual learning and growth. I savored this year, and determined somehow to reach religious perfection. My relationship with superiors was always deferential. Most of these women were wonderful role models. I also enjoyed my companions, although I hated recreation. I never enjoyed games, cards, crocheting, or any of the other acceptable forms of recreation.

My three and a half years in formation were spent at our motherhouse. I lived in a group of six, three team members and three initial formation people. We went to mass and breakfast with the motherhouse group. We had classes and cleaning duties. We lived in private rooms, could sign out cars for grocery shopping and doctors appointments. I saw a psychotherapist weekly. It was not my idea.

The community I entered had a formation program in transition. I was given private singing lessons though my other classes were with the other novices. I got along well with the mistress. We were her first group of novices. I enjoyed the novitiate. I wanted to chant the office, sing, pray, study, and that's what we did. I missed my friends from college very much, and I hated the outfits we had to wear. I also disliked it when the mistress took away our radios because a few of the novices were playing rock music at inappropriate times.

The first post-Vatican II chapter was held during our novitiate years. The community made every attempt to keep us from knowing what was going on. They didn't

want us contaminated by radical ideas. We used to steal
position papers from the retired sisters' bulletin board
in order to find out what was going on in the community.
The habit was the hot issue.

My preparation for the work I was to do for the community was excellent. I was sent to the best school.
I enjoyed the decency and goodness of my fellow novices.
I liked their genuine unselfishness and quick wits, sensitivity and depth. That kind of companionship is hard to
find. I disliked the confinement, the lack of physical
exercise, and the lack of close personal relationships.

We all tended to accept the restrictions, discipline,
and goofiness of the postulancy and novitiate. It was
not geared to help us mature. Studies and reading were
frowned upon as leading to intellectual pride. I found
this very hard. Recreation was enforced jollification.
Since we hardly knew what was going on in the outside
world, we had no topics for conversation. Minor events
took on great importance. We had to acknowledge our
faults publicly. I thought it was a waste of time and
a phony exercise because our sense of self worth was
already zero. Why humiliate us more? I liked my companions, and made lifelong friends. There were many happy
moments, some unforgettable Christmas and Easter
liturgies, some deep sharing with peers and with the
novice mistress. There was also a lot of loneliness.
As a second-year novice, I was sent out to teach at
a mission where the superior had a reputation for training
novices. She was a petty tyrant. I refused to toady to
her as the others did, and she recommended that I not
be permitted to make vows with my group. I had to
wait an extra year. My family never knew of my pain
and hurt.

As a postulant, I attended college full time, and had cleaning duties after classes. There was too much food. We were required to empty the serving platters at each table. Resistance was met with sanctions such as kneeling at table, banishment to another room, verbal harassment. I gained several pounds. As novices we spent our time in kitchen duties, cleaning, transplanting areas of the yard, sweeping the road, etc. My relationship with my superior was terrible. She was a perfect drill instructor. She singled me out early as a special target because I expressed some disapproval of the way in which she dealt with a nervous breakdown patient. My companions were younger, and eager to please the mistress. Knowing she disliked me, they avoided me. The few who became friends of mine were accused of particular friendship. They are my friends still. Our religious training was minimal.

Our novice mistress lost her mind during my thirty months as her prisoner. It was an intriguing spectacle. I was so interested in observing the progression of her insanity, that I failed to notice how unhappy I was. I fainted nearly every morning. I persevered to my profession day to spite her. She had done several things to try to get me to leave, and I was determined to stay.

III. Please Describe Your Community.

The community was founded to teach the children of the poor. By the time I entered, the sisters were teaching the middle class in long-established parochial schools and high schools. The spirit was one of simplicity. The sisters were relaxed, spontaneous, and humorous. There were some women of genuinely deep spirituality and holiness, but they would have been like that no matter where they were.

My community pivoted around the recitation of the office. The members were largely middle-class white. We served all classes.

The community was a mixture of old world and new. Some of the nuns were highly educated, and some were ordinary small-town women, just like me. We served the middle class, never the poor, hungry, or troubled. The community was devoted to the liturgy, and our teachers were thorough. The community was naive about many things. The perspective was out of kilter.

My community's only work was teaching. Our prayer was the divine office. We came from the middle class, and we served the middle class. Most of us were of German descent. Thinking about the community makes me ache. Tradition was an anchor that kept it from progress. I wished I had become a Carmelite instead.

The order sustained itself by the rosary, quaint prayers from the nineteenth century, readings from Thomas à Kempis, etc. The members were from lower and middle classes. Their virtues were simplicity and willingness to serve the poor. The failures were in the areas of education and keeping up with what was going on in other communities. Our community isolated itself completely until that could no longer be maintained. I never wished I had chosen a different order.

The members were mostly of German or Italian descent. The mother superior held absolute power. She remained

in office long after the constitutions allowed. Our sisters
served all classes of people. Most of the members of
the community came from middle and lower class families. Some came from broken homes seeking security
and status. Some entered to have material things impossible to get at home. This was during the Depression.
I never thought of another order after I entered. I kept
thinking we would improve.

I entered a large community. There were about sixty
in every reception class. Most of the sisters were middle
class, of German descent. We had a few Latin American
and Asian sisters. The few blacks felt uncomfortable,
and left. Our community was open and forward-looking
for the most part. We were among the first to modify
veils and habits.

Our community had over a thousand women. We were
teachers and nurses. Power was strictly vertical. Decisions were made at the top, and filtered down. Assignments were given, and no questions were asked. Exceptions were made for the friends of those in high places.
We were of Polish descent, from working class families.
I think we did a lot of good for the people we served,
but we were treated as robots. The superiors cared
more about the people we served than about us. We
were not helped to become fulfilled people. I never
thought of another order. I felt strong ties with those
with whom I experienced adversity. We always thought
things would get better.

The community was ruled by a mother general who
lived in Rome. Young girls were allowed to renounce
a life they had never experienced.

I entered a large community of teachers, nurses, domestics, missionaries, and social workers. We did not pray the office, but had litanies, the rosary, spiritual reading (Tanqueray), and examens. My community's chief virtues were friendliness and an openness to new apostolates before those things became commonplace. We weren't into deprivation. We had many parties and picnics. I never wished I had gone to another order.

The community's virtues were perseverance and strength. We failed to care adequately for the poor. I never thought of another order.

The spirit of the community was not a joyful one. There were times, feast days for instance, when there was joy, but it would be subdued by the superior. She believed in the traditional denials of religious life. The rule was all important, and took precedence over helping others. The power structure was autocratic, and everyone was afraid of the superior. Most of the nuns came from educated families, and were somewhat sophisticated, although some learned this in the community. These nuns always had trouble because they were put down by the superior, and they developed even more insecurities than the rest of us. All were white. Any black who came did not stay. We were good teachers because we had no social obligations to prevent us from spending our evenings making lesson plans. The community's failings were its use of guilt tactics to force people to obey, its teaching that the body was inferior and must be ignored, and the lack of human contact and relationships. I wished I had chosen a different community, but I felt I must stick it out.

In the province I entered, there were over a thousand sisters. The principal work was teaching. All policies were centered around teaching. Dedication to the poor was in our constitutions, but much work among the rich continued. The members were mostly Irish. A few Italians entered, but found it difficult to be accepted. Those elected to office generally went from one position to another. New people rarely were admitted to the circle of authority, no matter how capable. It was really a popularity contest at election time.

We had strong devotion to Our Lady. We were ruled by a mother general who lived in France. We were supposed to serve the poor, but most of our schools were in middle-class neighborhoods. Most of the members came from the middle class, and were of German and Irish descent. Our virtues, according to lay people, were serenity and happiness. To me, they were the kindness and respect with which we treated one another.

Our community imbibed the spirit of its founder, a priest trained in Jansenism, gloom and sin. When I entered, there were over a thousand sisters. We taught in middle-class schools and in academies for the affluent.

Our community was founded in Germany. It was originally semi-cloistered. We were primarily teachers, but were beginning to look into other areas. We served all classes. I loved the community, and still do. I never regretted choosing it.

My community was large. It had schools across the country, academies, hospitals, colleges, the works. Very successful. The community had been directed for years by a talented superior, widely known. The spirit of the community was typical of the American church at the time, traditional, and subservient to the bishops. The leaders of our community put more emphasis on intellectual life than did the male hierarchy. Nearly every sister with intellectual or artistic skills was encouraged to develop it at the best schools. I was proud to be a member of my community, and felt it was the most progressive in terms of encouraging an independent spirit, and allowing intellectual growth.

My community was founded in Germany, and most of the nuns were from German, middle-class backgrounds, work-oriented, super-clean, and old-fashioned. When I entered in 1974, the average age was sixty-eight. Many feared and resented education. Some were racists. Some despised members of their own sex and indulged priests. We were good nurses. Professionalism in our hospitals was the goal of those under fifty. I loved being part of the community.

There were three hundred and fifty nuns in the community I entered. We chanted the divine office in common, and taught full time. There were over forty women with doctorates, many more with master's degrees. Many were successful writers, painters, translators, educators, photographers, musicians. With so many articulate and powerful people, life can be difficult for everyone for reasons that are obvious. I never wished I had chosen a different order.

My community had five thousand members. We worked in schools at all levels, in hospitals, and in other institutions. There were strict rules about home visits, speaking on the street, in bedrooms, corridors, etc. We greeted one another with a short ejaculation which was answered with Amen. A silent nun was considered a good nun. I now realize that we had nothing to say, and were uncreative, dull, morose, and without humor. We spent many hours in prayer, more than any community that was not cloistered. This created a pressure of time, because we had to prepare classes, attend to housecleaning, study, and attend to parish chores. Many slept soundly at morning meditation. We served all classes. We came from the middle class. College graduates who entered with a degree were handled with kid gloves. The spirit of individual houses in those pre-Vatican II days depended on the personality of the superior. Her influence was absolute.

There were four hundred in the community. The superior was into Sister Formation. She was determined to return sisters to discipline, prayer, and obedience. She was superior, and others listened. She made all decisions. She did not have a reputation for having a heart.

IV. Please Tell About Your Life as a Professed Sister.

I was sent to a college for nuns only. It was pitiful. Various communities sent their junior sisters there, and we were in class together, but we were not allowed to talk to each other outside class. There was a great fear that sisters from one community could somehow contaminate sisters from another. It was a brave sight to see the hundreds of young nuns in their beautiful habits. It was in the early 1960s, and the juniorates were overflowing. My companions and I felt that our community didn't need us in its schools, so they sent us to this make-believe college to keep us out of the way. The older sisters in our community didn't attend this school. They went to universities. But they resented us for getting to go to school full time instead of going straight to the missions as they did.

Teaching was very difficult. I hated it. I was very immature, I was reassigned every couple of years. No promotions. No vacations. Until the late 1960s, we weren't allowed to enter our parents' homes. The happiest time was the summer we changed from the Latin office to English. We reproduced and collated books all summer. The most unhappy time was the year before final vows. After much counseling, I decided to stay. I was considered a loner.

We juniors were treated as second class citizens, kept from knowing what was going on in the community. We worked in the large convent where the perpetually professed sisters came and went all summer. We cleaned up and made beds. With each other we were always afraid of becoming too close. Always walk with three or more, they warned us. My most unhappy time was on a mission when I was assigned to be the cook even though I knew nothing about cooking. Teaching all day and cooking all evening. It was a time of great stress. My prayer life had no meaning. I preferred a quiet, wordless kind of prayer, but I was ordered to say the community prayers, and obey the meaningless rules. The harsh reality began to dawn. I could not grow or be myself in the midst of so many unhappy, underdeveloped people.

I taught chemistry and physics in high school for twenty-five years. I received a master's degree in chemistry from Catholic University.

After profession, I was missioned. I worked on getting my degree every summer. It took me ten years. We got up early in the morning, slept during chapel, had breakfast together, taught school all day. After school we corrected papers and planned lessons until spiritual reading time. After that we had chapel, supper, recreation, then bed. Then get up and begin it all over again. I still know a couple of hundred women who feel very satisfied doing this, but I don't know why. The food and medical care were excellent. Every summer we went to the motherhouse for summer school and retreat. This was the happy time because you would see your friends. We were allowed to visit home every year. Assignments were like a checkers game: Every move made another move necessary until all the slots were filled. We existed to fill slots. It didn't do much for community life on the missions or for personal stability. Assignments were given out in a barbaric way. All the sisters would gather in the auditorium. We would be given mimeographed booklets which contained the names of the schools and lists of the sisters who would be teaching at each one. With pounding heart you would look first to the school you had taught at the previous year. If your name wasn't there, you knew you had been uprooted once again. Then you had to look through the entire list to find your assignment.

I was sent to teach in a two-room school. I loved it. I prepared my classes as if it were Harvard. I became obsessed with my kids. The nun who was principal of the little school required me to submit my lesson plans to her. Sometimes she would steal them. I would walk into her classroom after lunch, and start to teach. Her

kids would say, "Sister already told us that this morning."
She read my mail, and withheld anything she wanted,
magazines and so forth. I taught religion to public school
kids two nights a week, and was constantly on call to
drive the motherhouse nuns to the chiropractor. I was
in charge of the sacristy at the little parish where I
worked. I was tired all the time. I started skipping meals
and prayers. It was only in the classroom that I was
alive.

My unhappiness began in the juniorate. The silence
and monastic observance were of a lower quality than
they had been in the novitiate. I loved the community,
and was disturbed by the infractions of the rule. I was
disturbed also by the increasing intensity of my sexual
feelings. Older nuns sought friendships on vacations,
but I was looking for maternal warmth and they were
moved by sexual frustration. They were masculine and
aggressive. The order's injunctions against particular
friendship confused the issue. I felt that I was in more
danger from other women in the convent than I had
been from men on the outside. I wanted to be a hermit,
or a clown you could joke with but never get close to.
Once I went to tell the news of a death to an older
nun. I thought she would be studying or sleeping or reading
or praying. She was lying on her bed with earphones
on and liquor on her breath. The fact that she could
listen to the radio after the Great Silence was too much.
I couldn't understand why the order tolerated laxity
among the professed, but forced the novices to live
like Trappists.

I was appointed organist and choir director even though
I had no musical ability. Local superiors would declare
that this or that whim or fancy was God's will. Some
would be very hard on the housekeeper if the evening
meal was three minutes late. Sometimes we borrowed

cars from parishioners, who then sacrificed their own convenience. We went to bed at 9:30 even though there were hungry people in town and lonely people.

The food was always sufficient and of good quality. I had no vacations, although occasionally I visited my family. Particular friendships were discouraged, but being a normal human, I felt a need for close relationships with certain people, and I usually found the courage to pursue them, even though I encountered rebukes from superiors. I was a local superior once, and held office in the community twice.

We were expected to behave submissively to priests. When Forty Hours was held at the convent, dozens of priests would come to celebrate. Afterwards they sat at table in the opulent priests' dining room while the nuns served them. No one ever said, why don't we celebrate together? The pastor at the school where I was principal despised me, and criticized me to the community and parents. One Saturday I went over to the school, and found that he had unlocked my office door, and was going through my desk drawers. From that day until the end of the year he refused to speak to me. He withheld the final pay checks from the lay teachers, and told them to sue. They came to me for help, and I was helpless.

I was sent out to teach first and second grade. I had fifty-five children in my class. I had no idea, other than my own experience in first grade, of what to do. I wasn't allowed to see my classroom until the day before school started. The superior told us not to speak to the pastor unless he spoke to us first, and then to answer briefly.

In that diocese, teachers were required to have credentials, so some were sent in for us who had none doctored
to fit the situation. Besides teaching, I had church work
to do, cooking, cleaning, laundry (which we got up at
three o'clock to do), and hours of prayer. Another young
nun and I would ask permission to go to confession (which
we knew couldn't be denied) to get a chance to take
a walk. We would walk to the farthest church. I felt
it was unfair to the parents and children to be teaching
without preparation. I was sent to summer school at
Catholic University to study primary education. My
mother was killed the first summer, and the community
made me stay in school, and not go to her funeral since
my family couldn't pay my ticket. (It was the early
1930s.) That fall I was sent to Hawaii. When I got there,
I learned I was assigned to teach in high school, a subject
I had never studied, to supervise boarders, and to take
care of housekeeping. I was twenty-one. I had my birthday
on the ship en route to Hawaii. All of the other sisters
were over fifty. I made final vows in Hawaii. I cried
after saying my vows. The nuns thought it was because
I missed my companions. I began to take correspondence
courses from a college in the states. There was a university within walking distance of our convent, but I was
not permitted to go there. After fifteen years, I received
a B.A. Our food was not nutritional. This took its toll
on my teeth. My students liked me, and I had a good
relationship with my superiors and sisters. I was a
local superior, high school principal, and member of
the council at various times.

In our cloistered community we kept perpetual silence
except for a half hour of recreation when we could
speak only to the superior. Our time was spent in manual
labor and in our cells where we sewed relic cases, and
unwound string to make thread. The string came from
grocery packages. The superior and most of the nuns
were in ill health.

I was treated like a baby. The older nuns on my mission pushed me around and criticized me, but I made some lifelong friends among the nuns who were my age. (They have all left, too.) My principals and superiors picked on me, and I was transferred every year or two until the new changes came in. Then we had lots of discussions. Emotions were high on the part of the older nuns who didn't want any changes. I was helped to regain a sense of self worth by a kind and brilliant nun from another community who lived at our convent while attending a university.

I taught school during the year, and attended college in the summer. It took me ten years to get a degree. The food was adequate, but the dentist who donated his services was not very good. We were allowed to visit our parents for five days every five years. We were given our assignments on August fifteenth every year. The younger sisters in particular were changed often. Our superiors were strict, and enforced the most insignificant regulations. Relationships were discouraged. Our mail was read, and telephone calls were restricted. Friendships had to be made and maintained in covert ways. The happy times were holidays, feastdays, the occasional movie, visits from parents. The unhappy times were spent on missions where the superior was particularly tough, and the other sisters older than I. I was considered something of a goof-off because I disregarded incidental regulations when charity to others was at stake. I was always reliable about my work. Some of the sisters liked me because I was a champion of the underdogs. Others, especially superiors, disliked me, probably because they considered me a threat to a tightly run ship.

Vatican II brought changes. We were allowed to have friends, and we looked at our lifestyle with critical

eyes for the first time. I was transferred in the middle
of a school year because I refused to teach the sacrament
of penance to second graders.

I went to our community's college after profession.
The quality of education was good to excellent. Life
in the juniorate was the same as the novitiate except
that we had more freedom, and recreation was more
stimulating. We had movies, plays, concerts, recitals,
etc. This was a very happy time for me. In 1962 I was
sent on mission. I was not trusted by the superior and
the older sisters. I was ten years younger than the next
youngest sister. The older nuns resented me because
I had a degree, and they were still working on theirs
in summer school. There were many misfits in the community, and I couldn't understand how the community
allowed them to get away with open temper tantrums,
not speaking to one another for years sometimes, and
possessing money and expensive gifts. From 1963 through
1972 I lived in various houses where life ranged from
acceptable to comfortable. I was well liked, and had
many friends in and out of the community. I had a reputation for not putting up with unacceptable behavior which
made me unpopular with the crazies. In 1972 with four
others, I went into small group living. We rented a house
and all worked in different places. We were given the
community's blessing, but no financial help. There were
many such groups at the time. It was the happiest time.

I was a junior for two years. It was wonderful. A grand
gal was the mistress. We had very strong ties as a group.
The junior mistress was the first formation person to
treat us as individuals and not as plaster-cast nuns.
She encouraged us to think, and this led to problems.
When we went on mission, the sisters weren't prepared
for us or we for them. We were too idealistic, and the
reality of mission life really disillusioned us. Ten of

my classmates left during their first year out of the
juniorate. I liked the summer months best. We went
to St. Louis University, and the freedom away from
the community was great. So was the academic atmosphere, and being with friends. I was sent to teach high
school. During a teachers' strike, I sided with the lay
teachers. All of us who were in sympathy with the strikers
and against the sister superior were sent to different
missions far away. I was disillusioned and furious. My
image in the community was that of a radical. I challenged authority figures, and headed up our peace and
justice committee. I picketed for farm workers, and
worked for ecology. I was frustrated over the compla-
cency of the people I lived with, and very lonely.

Medical care was only for the asking. A good sister
put up with illness. I was never taken to a gynecologist.
I had a yeast infection for several years, but I was afraid
to ask to go. We were required to write home every
week, and the mother superior read the letters. We
were subjected to degrading treatment, public punish-
ment, etc. I was happy in college, but the superior felt
I was becoming too attached to my studies. I don't know
how the others regarded me. Everyone was so screwed
up that no one had a realistic picture of anyone else.
I think people either liked me or were jealous of me.
Sometimes I felt at home, but never comfortable since
I was not allowed to make decisions about my life.

I was missioned directly from the novitiate. I worked
in social service for five years, but the work was too
stressful for me. My health deteriorated. After a long
and difficult struggle with the community, I was allowed
to go back to school to study another field. A former
superior told me the community was not getting its
money's worth out of me. I expected support, caring,
and concern in community life, but I didn't find it.

———————————

I taught in four schools in thirteen years. In the summer I went to school. The food was always good, and medical care was available. We had no vacations. A change was as good as a vacation, we were told. I had some very close friends in the community, and none on the outside.

———————————

I was assigned to study nursing. I found I liked it, and did very well in my studies. After graduation, I was assigned to the operating room. My forte was administration. I was well liked by the physicians and nurses. My superior did not like this, and made life quite difficult. I received a government scholarship, and went to study nursing education. There was little consultation with me about this. I was told to major in supervision of orthopedics. I learned to like this field, and after graduation was assigned to set up the first orthopedic unit in our hospital. I developed a program which attracted more and more nurses. We had an excellent esprit-de-corps. This was a source of great satisfaction to me. The patients and their families benefitted from the good care we provided. While ostensibly happy and respected, I felt that something was missing. I lived with five sisters, but always had a feeling of anomie. I craved something, but wasn't sure what it was. Some of the doctors and priests and male patients let me know that they had affectionate feelings about me, but even platonic friendship with males was looked at critically. I found this difficult. I was ignorant sexually. I knew anatomy and physiology, but the nuances of love were a mystery.

———————————

In my first year after profession I lived with another junior and a mother mistress. We were happy and outgoing. We went to school full time, taught C.C.D., tutored in the inner city, and worked in a nursing home. I was happy that year. We prayed together, shared our hopes and dreams, and I was appreciated. Then in 1970 everything changed. We had our first modern retreat. It touched on problems that had been buried, but were festering. Everything changed. The juniorate was done away with. We moved in small groups into apartments. Collegiality was the word. Many left at this time, five in one week once. We were to be self-supporting. We hardly ever came together for meals or prayer. Within months there were many problems. After I finished my B.A., I was sent to a foreign mission. There were nuns from five different cultures in our group of eight. It was absurd. I returned to the U.S. My culture shock coming back was worse than going out. I was confused and unhappy. My health deteriorated.

I was sent out to teach sixth grade. It was too much for me, and I was given fourth grade. Our superior-principal was a saintly woman, but very ill. It was a large house with multiple problems, including a power struggle. I was extremely rigid at the time. If a rule existed, I saw it as unbendable. I was upset by the politics and by those ready for Vatican II before John XXIII.

I was professed at the age of seventeen. I was sent to teach in an elementary school. I taught from 1953 to 1968. My assignment was considered a plum. I went to summer school at Catholic University. I had a reputation as a scholar. I received a scholarship to a European university, and received consistent praise for papers and articles I wrote or delivered. I was made to understand that I would teach in a university. I was elected to our general chapter. I was conservative, as was our community. There was never enough time to study, and I had some superiors I disliked, but for the most

part I was happy. My personal needs were amply met,
and I was respected and treated well. I had a few close
friends. When I began graduate school in 1962, I came
in contact with people who challenged my narrow view
of the world. I began to get involved in the civil rights
movement.

I loved being part of the community. I made waves,
supported E.R.A., left off my veil, urged attention
to social justice issues, called for women's ordination.
I had learned in the novitiate that it's okay to touch
and hug, that I had lots of sexual fears, that it's okay
to cry, that other people can't read my mind, and that
give and take is necessary on a daily basis. Now I had
one hundred grandmas telling me how to dress, how
to walk, when to be quiet. I complied partially, but
inside I struggled. I enjoyed the older sisters, and my
work and friends. But I knew I was hiding, and I got
sick.

Because of my easy going temperament and sensitivity
toward others, I was very much liked. Many local communities asked for me to be assigned to them. I genuinely
liked my community, and felt very much at home in
it.

I loved teaching, especially junior high. I was transferred
after one year to another house, but I got sick. I was
allergic to the mold in the convent. I got involved in
the charismatic movement. For the first time since
grade school, I felt the presence of God. It was very
good. But the community was suspicious of its charismatic
nuns running off every evening to meetings with lay
men and women. In addition, the pastor tried to run

the school through intimidation. I refused to be intimi-
dated, or to let him intimidate my seventh graders.
In the middle of the year, he asked that I be removed
from the school. I went back to the motherhouse. Several
of our schools had openings, but they all refused to
take me. Finally I was assigned to a new school, the
best the community had. It was a very affirming warm
fuzzy from the community.

I expected to find in religious life much sharing on a
deeply spiritual level, and I did not find it. Decay had
set in, and the life had become rigid and deadly.

I was sent to our private school after profession. I was
treated well for the most part by my superiors. I had
many enjoyable evenings bantering with the other nuns.
We played tennis, rode bikes and felt happy that we
were serving God in a special way. There was one unhappy
time, a brief homosexual situation. Religious life turned
out to be much as I expected. The camaraderie and
goodness of my fellow nuns were more than I had antici-
pated. My image was that of a dependable, hardworking,
decent, and kindly person who liked to have a good
time. I felt very much at home and secure.

I loved most of my colleagues, but liked only two out
of seven superiors. The major superiors chose local
superiors who were yes-women, who did not have independent thoughts, and were easily controlled. I taught first
grade for eight years, and hated every minute of it.
One thing good came out of it. I came to understand
small children, and still can speak their language. But
it was intellectually stultifying, and physically draining.
My community was (and is) strong in prayer, in working

hard, and in taking pains. Most of the nuns are compassionate, self-sacrificing, and gentle. But they failed to let us develop. This resulted in bitterness, alienation, and pain for many. Uniformity was a virtue. It was destructive to give people assignments without consultation. For instance, I was assigned to get an M.A. in a foreign language even though I would have preferred English. My undergraduate degree was in English, but the community needed language teachers. I was happy on the days I made first and final vows, when my family visited me, when I spent summers at our vacation house with other sisters, and one summer when I won a scholarship to study in Europe. I was most unhappy when I was transferred—more than once—at a superior's whim from a house where I had friends and was enjoying success and fulfillment. I do not wish I had chosen a different order, but today I'm not sure if I would have entered in the first place.

I was sent on a large mission with an old and senile superior. When someone disagreed with her or threatened to mention her craziness to the mother superior, she would become ill. Then the pastor would be summoned to administer extreme unction. We would kneel all night in her bedroom and at her door, praying, waiting for her to die. She would recover the next morning, and we would go to our classrooms, having gone without sleep. It was an effective means of government. Once she told me to cook dinner. I had never cooked a meal for twenty-five people, and there was no recipe book in the house. (Our regular cook who was ill cooked by memory.) I found a recipe for tuna casserole on the back of a potato chip bag. That's what I made, tuna a potato chip casseroles. The nuns loved it.

V. Why Did You Leave the Convent?

I met two men who were living the kind of religious
life I wanted. They had come together to seek God.
They had settled on a plot of land, and were seeking
God with their whole lives. I visited their little shack
with a sister who is still my friend and theirs. We sat
around the pot-bellied stove and talked about philosophy,
poetry, and literature. They were alive with ideas and
convictions. I felt happy and alive for the first time.
I thought maybe it wasn't my fault that I didn't fit in
at the convent. I made the decision to leave the convent
and join the men.

In the 1960s in Central America, change was in the
works as it was back home. Our Jesuit friends were
going through changes as were our sisters. Many of
our older sisters were disturbed. We were young and
full of ideas that frightened them, and which they did
not want to hear. I fell in love with a Jesuit scholastic.
I felt an intellectual attraction, an emotional attraction,
a comradeship of souls, and physical attraction. The
single most disturbing thing about Central America
was the contrast of lifestyle between the nuns and the
people whom we were serving. We had everything and
they had nothing. The excuse we used was we need
all this to be healthy and to do our work. It was a shocking
joke. My feelings about the man I loved and my confusion
about poverty disturbed my thoughts and my sleep.
When it came time to make final vows, I flew back
to the motherhouse and renewed my vows for one year.
Many of my companions were leaving, and one said
she would leave when she got her doctorate. I felt like
a traitor to God and myself. Leaving was one of the
most difficult things I have ever done. I was leaving
people I loved, the man I loved, the country I loved.

What was I going back to? My parents were alcoholics. I was a stranger to my brothers and sisters. I would have been a hypocrite to make final vows. I hated myself. I felt like a failure.

Celibacy was an issue for me. I missed male companionship. I was blamed for things and money that disappeared. My psychologist kept reassuring me that I wasn't crazy, but the circumstances around me were. His advice: leave!

I left the convent because I couldn't stand it any longer. I was nervous and often ill. For five years I pondered it. One year when I asked to leave, the mother superior asked me to stay one more year. She needed us so badly. I agreed, and stayed three more years. But I needed to look forward to something. All I had to look forward to was teaching little kids the rest of my life. Even my vocabulary was on an elementary school level. I did not really enjoy teaching. I would rather have been a nurse. I would probably still be a nun if they had loosened some of the rules like never going anywhere alone.

I began to think about leaving in the novitiate, but had no one to talk to. In the juniorate, I told the superior I wanted to leave, but I stayed. I might have stayed longer if the community had decided to modernize a little faster. Even when they advanced a little, they then regressed a lot. Finally I told the superior I was leaving. I am sure she was relieved. I had been advised by my spiritual director to get counseling. As a result, I began changing from the shy reserved person I had been to an outspoken and assertive one. I left the convent when I was able to have good feelings about myself.

The years in the convent took a physical toll. I was on nine different medications, but quit them all when I left the convent.

———————

God is as close to us as we can risk being close to our real selves. The convent was filled with people who seemed to be moving farther and farther away from themselves. The convent lifestyle was inhumane. I discussed my real reasons for leaving with the mother general and the novice mistress. My physical and mental states were excellent. I felt strong within, but sad about leaving the community I had loved for so many years.

———————

I was overburdened with a variety of different assignments on a community level and as a college administrator. I was turned off by the emphasis on non-essentials. I was put down when I tried to help solve certain community problems. I told the prioress and a close friend I was leaving. They discouraged me, and I postponed my decision. Later, however, I felt I should seek a dispensation. I received it without difficulty. I didn't stay longer than I wanted to. I was not sent for psychological counseling. My physical state was good, and I felt pretty good about myself as I prepared to leave.

———————

I started to have dreams and fantasies about my eighth grade boys. I knew it was time to go. I stopped going to community exercises, and I stopped eating. (I had gained thirty pounds in my years in the convent.) The superior begged me to stay one more year, and I did. It was 1964 when I told her I wanted to leave. The talk

was about changing the habit, and I couldn't stand it.
The anger and ill will on the part of those who didn't
want to change shocked me. They hissed at the others,
and criticized them for things that seemed incredible—
chewing gum, crossing the knees, etc. Finally I realized
God couldn't possibly care about the things MEN had
decided we should do—hide beneath yards of fabric,
dress alike, cut our hair. It covered lots of deep-seated
sexual problems. It was so sick. I couldn't wait to be
free but at the same time I felt like Judas.

I left the convent only because my mother died suddenly,
and I am an only child. My father is not a Catholic,
so when he went into a deep depression, my superiors
recommended I take a leave of absence. After a year,
I renewed it for another year. With all the changes
and mixed-up conditions within the community, I felt
I could serve God just as well outside. After twenty-five
years of religious life, I was experiencing so many doubts
about the order's commitment and its practices that
I determined to leave.

I probably thought about leaving from the first day,
but I always had the hope that things would get better.
People spouted idealistic comments at meetings, and
then did the opposite in daily life. I worked twenty-
three years non-stop. We gave all our money to needy
projects. Any suggestion to make provision for our retirement was voted down. Some sisters gave up the struggle,
and left. I was tired, and wanted to make decisions
for myself. I left in 1980. Everyone was very nice. They
expressed disappointment, and said they wished I would
stay. I was not advised to seek spiritual direction, and
I did not. I was healthy, but very tired.

Nine years after entering, I left. I came to realize that
I hadn't been mature enough at seventeen to make the
decision I did, to renounce a life I had never experienced.
I began thinking when John XXIII opened the windows
to let in openness, honest discussion, and criticism.
I was not advised to seek counsel. I didn't stay longer
than I wanted to. I talked about my real reasons for
leaving. I was emotionally and physically well at the
time I left.

I left the convent because I could no longer live the
vows. I wanted money, a love life, and initiative in
my own life. I began thinking about leaving in 1970.
I told my superiors in 1974. They told me I had to have
documentation of counseling before my dispensation
would be granted, but they accepted counseling I had
been in prior to telling them. I felt very good about
myself, and was in excellent physical health.

My superiors advised me to see a psychiatrist, but he
was one they had chosen. I don't believe in psychiatry,
and even if I did, how could I trust someone they had
hired not to report to them what I said? How could
a man understand a woman's problems? How could a
Cuban understand an American's problems? How could
a layman understand a nun's problems? How could someone whose "science" taught that women suffered from
"penis envy" understand anything?

I began thinking about leaving in the postulancy, but
the mistress assured me I belonged in the convent. I
struggled each time I made vows. I couldn't bring myself
to make final vows. Two years earlier I had met and
fallen in love with a priest. It was a mutual situation,

and for the first time I have a realization that I might be happy with a family. I wanted to marry him. My home life had been lousy, but he had had such a wonderful family life that I began to see it as an option. I told the superior I was leaving. She cried, but was supportive, and did not try to sway me. My spiritual director advised me to seek counsel. I did, but the psychiatrist was more disturbed than I was.

Immediately after final vows I knew I had made a mistake. I knew I had been pressured into going ahead, and I knew there was nothing for me in religious life. I learned this attitude from my friends in graduate school and from one teacher in particular who showed me that the spiritual life is strengthened and enhanced by contact with others, not weakened. I began to see the importance of healthy relationships, and friendship and human love, all lacking in the convent. I discussed my feelings with one other sister. She tried to convince me to stay.

I started noticing the differences between the people inside and outside the community. The nuns were selfish, uncaring, and unprayerful. I left at age twenty-nine after ten years in the community. The community's ministry to the rich turned me off. So did hair coloring, earrings, smoking, and drinking. It was 1982.

I left because I wanted to run my own life and because I did not want to be put on a shelf in old age. I asked to leave a couple of times, but was convinced to stay.

I left the convent because of feeling unimportant as
an individual. I felt loved by the community in the ab-
stract, but not as a person. I felt that if I died, their
only reaction would be the need to get rid of the body.
I had no real bonds. I felt no affection. I felt this way
for years, but when I spoke to priests about it, they
always said I had a vocation. Also, I was afraid my leaving
would make my mother feel bad. I stuck it out year
after year even though I was being intellectually dishon-
est. I began to see a psychiatrist. He told me I was
normal, but not facing reality. At that time, I was sent
out to a foreign mission. When I returned after two
years, I decided to leave. I knew I had another twenty
or thirty years left to live, and I did not want to live
it unhappily.

I was very happy, but I knew that not every mission
was like the one I was on. I felt I needed roots. Being
uprooted every year or two was more than I could endure.
About this time I began to want to have children of
my own. I told a friend, my confessor, and a former
superior that I was leaving. They were all most supportive.

The community sent me to London to get a doctorate.
I decided I would not return after I finished my dissertation. I told no one. When I returned, I asked the mother
superior for a leave of absence. She was very understanding, and said the community would help me any way
it could. She gave me $1000. The community was in
the throes of finding a new identity in the post-Vatican
II world, and was moving too slowly for me. I was tired
of the endless discussions about the habit, community
life, and prayer. I had begun to view many of the nuns
as mediocre. The most talented were leaving. By 1971
there was little holding me. I was also interested in
men. I found men far more interesting to spend time
with than women. I talked to a couple of my married

friends about what a thirty-five year old ex-nun could
do to find a man.

My old anger at my family erupted, and I became suicidal.
I worked with a counselor. At one point I overdosed
on pills. The sisters were very kind and supportive.
No gossip or bitching. A lot of advice to relax and stop
working so hard. But I was subtly urged to leave.

I had to leave because I didn't belong there any more.
It seems simplistic, but it is the truth. I believe I was
called to that particular community for some particular
reason. I know that being there gave me many things,
and I believe I left behind many positive gifts to them.
I became critically ill, and the weeks in the hospital
gave me plenty of time to think. After leaving the hospital, I went to my parents' house for more rest. I knew
then that it was over. I visited the motherhouse to inform
the superior that I was leaving. She was terribly shocked,
but most kind and generous.

I was asked to teach fourth grade instead of eighth.
I made it clear that I was not willing to make the change.
The superior told me I had to teach the grade given
me or leave. I chose to leave. I was the new administration's test case to demonstrate to the nuns that they
had to stay in the classroom.

I did not want to leave my order. I was pressured out
because of the fear my superiors had of anyone who
spoke out for change. Spiritual direction was not avail-

able. Psychology, which major superiors had become
aware of in the 1950s and 1960s, was a deadly weapon
in the hands of some.

Most of those who entered with me had left. I was assigned to a job I considered boring and unchallenging.
I had begun to experience the need for close physical
love. I was forced to make a decision. The superior
told me on the phone to accept a new assignment or
leave. I told her I would leave. She told me to pray
over it. I saw an outstanding psychologist—Jewish.
He helped me get in touch with my feelings. I felt shaky
and uncertain about how to manage the transition. I
was physically strained, and emotionally upset.

VI. How Did Others in the Community Treat You When It Became Known You Were Leaving?

I was local superior at several missions over the years.
Sometimes I was sent to straighten up situations where
other superiors had allowed dreadful conditions to develop. I was junior mistress for a time, and a department
chairman in our college. Then I attended a biblical insti-
tute. It was renewal, hope, life, health, normality. I
prayed to the God of Truth to help me. On the feast
of the Epiphany the idea came to me to leave. It grew
with great intensity, but an accreditation team was
coming to our college. I decided to wait until June.
That would cause the least disruption for the community,
the college, and the convent. To my surprise, early
in April, the superior called me, and told me to leave
the convent in two days. She said I had never had a
vocation at all. (I had been a member of the community
for thirty-five years.) She told me I must leave the
state. Two days later, I called the regional superior
from the airport. She asked if I was in the habit. (What

else did I have?) I said yes. She told me to change into secular clothes in the ladies' lavatory. (This was in a tiny airport in a small town.) I had no lay clothes to put on. I went to the regional convent. The superior handed me $100, the dowry I had brought to the convent. Then she said, "You must have sinned dreadfully for God to abandon you so." My hair was very short. The stores were closed. A friend took me to her apartment. Her family was gracious and unquestioning. The next day she took me to get a permanent and some clothing. I bought a ticket to the city where my brother lived. My brother and sister-in-law took me in. Their children asked me direct questions about what had happened. I answered directly. They never brought up the question again. I was fifty-four years old and in good health. A priest I knew spoke to my former superior. She told him I was possessed by the devil.

My best friend begged me to stay. Our community had a rule that said anyone who left could not communicate with any of the nuns for five years.

I left the convent after twelve years of teaching, and getting a degree. The community was open to my leaving, although I didn't share my real reasons with them. They gave me a $500 no interest loan.

I went to every one of the twelve sisters who lived in the convent with me, and tried to explain. I did this because I had seen sisters leave before, and it was all clouded in intrigue and mystery. Everyone knew something was going on, but the sister would just vanish one day. I didn't want them to remember me like that. They all told me they appreciated my candor, and each one

told me she would pray for me. I was very grateful
for that. In the months between opening up to them
and leaving, the sisters were wonderful to me. They
realized I was going through a hard time, and they wanted
to help. I returned to the motherhouse, and was hidden
in a little room by a grim old nun. In the morning she
brought my breakfast on a tray so I wouldn't be seen.
I was taken to the superior to sign the papers. I kept
worrying that something would go wrong, and I wouldn't
get to leave. (I had nightmares about that for years
afterward.) I went back to the little room and changed
clothes. I folded my habit, and left my ring and crucifix
in plain sight. I combed out my hair, and went to the
shopping center at the corner. It was like the first day
of my life. Everything seemed bathed in sunshine. The
sisters gave me $200.

———————

The sisters were extremely supportive. They had seen
so many leave already, that it was no big shock. It
was 1969. I was twenty-six. I had $100 and some clothing
from the poor box. I walked into my parents' house
for the first time in nine years. They said they'd be
down as soon as a commercial came on. I stayed with
them for two miserable weeks, and then went to New
York.

———————

A sister went with me to see a psychologist. They wanted
to have me placed in a mental hospital. They thought
I was crazy because I wanted to leave. I told them I
wasn't crazy, and my psychologist backed me up. I just
couldn't take the strain any more.

———————

No one knew I was leaving. I went to mass and prayers
with the sisters. After breakfast the mother general

and some of the council kissed me goodbye. I left through the front door. Two sisters drove me to my mother's house. I received my dowry back.

I was forty-five when I left in 1967. The sisters were very cordial and gracious. I was not aware of any bad feelings. I felt their blessing. The prioress and two other sisters took me to the airport. We had dinner there, and then I left. The community gave me airfare home and $50.

My brother drove down to pick me up. I was thirty-three. He fixed a flat tire for the nuns before we left. They gave us dinner. I never felt looked down on.

I left in 1980, aged forty-six. I had been living with another sister since 1970. (I still live with her.) All I did was sign my dispensation and stay where I was. The community permitted me to keep my car, the contemporary clothing I had, and the furniture in our house. I was permitted to keep a few months' salary from the previous year. I have no complaints.

When it became known I was leaving, the sisters who mattered to me gave me support. I left in 1969. The community returned my dowry, and gave me $300. I received neither letters of recommendation nor help with finding a job.

The day before I left the superior was crying and begging me to stay. (I had been teaching in a place no one else wanted.) The day I left, she took me down a back stairway, and saw me out the back door. I received no money. The superior agreed to write a letter of recommendation to the headmaster of the school where I would be teaching. (He told me a few months later that in her letter she said I was mentally ill.)

———————

I was given an adequate severance check. Our community was already in secular clothing, so I had a few things to wear. After I signed my dispensation, I was allowed into the cloister to conduct some business (I had been the bookkeeper), and to say goodbye. A sister and I went out to celebrate with dinner. (She left a few years later.)

———————

I told a few sisters I was leaving, and they were great, but I felt guilty about making them sad. It was the pits. I was afraid God would be displeased with me for leaving. I left in 1975. I was thirty. I left by the side door. I was numb, sad, scared, and relieved. The community lent me $2000 interest free, and gave me my dowry back.

———————

A sister discovered I was leaving, and wrote a very cruel note to me. I knew I couldn't wait any longer to leave. On the day I left, a friend said I could use her apartment. I had gotten some money from my parents. I had sent my books and papers to a friend's house. During the school day, I arranged for my class to be covered. I went back to the convent and got my things. I left in my habit since I wanted to avoid discovery. I left my cross and ring with a letter to the superior. I had bought some cheap clothes, and I had let my hair grow. Later, my community refused to return personal documents they had of mine—my birth certificate, diplomas, etc. I knew they would not help with money or letters of recommendation.

Friends on the outside helped me. I put up a note to the nuns I had been living with. I couldn't face telling each one individually. The community gave me $1200. I left in 1982 at the age of twenty-nine. I was psychologically exhausted.

There were so many leaving when I did—1968—that it was treated with resignation. I was thirty-two. The community gave me $300. I received a dispensation, and left by the front door. I went to live with a friend, another ex-nun.

The community gave me $1000. That was $500 more than they gave others. They said it was because I had served so long. The community had no idea of what it cost to buy clothes, to place a security deposit on an apartment, to buy furniture.

The sisters I was living with were most kind. They could tell I was having difficulties. On the other hand, the administration was very cold, legalistic, and not understanding of the financial situation I was in. They gave me $200. I had spent eleven years doing the community's work. A sister gave me $100 that her family had given her. It was against the rules. My last day was a difficult one. The sisters prepared a special prayer service. Then we had pizza—a real treat. It was an awkward time. I didn't sleep well that night.

The sisters were wonderful. I signed out of the community in July, but lived in the convent until September. The sisters collected items for my apartment. They gave me the bed, chair, and chest from my room. The pastor loaned me $300. I was thirty-one. It was 1970.

My friends in the community were wonderful. Everyone was kind and supportive. The community had been good to me. I had simply grown in a different way.

On the morning I left there were gifts in the mailbox. My last letter from the provincial spoke of the possibility of return.

My community gave me a large check, and was most supportive in every way. Everyone was upset, and some cried. Everyone continued to be loving and supportive.

The community gave me no money. I had one dollar left from the $25 monthly allowance we received. I made a dress from an old habit. I wanted to stay at the motherhouse while I looked for a job, but the superior sent me a telegram giving me twenty-four hours to get out. Another community allowed me to stay at their motherhouse. My former community at this point gave me $75.

Others in the community were sad to see me go. In some eyes I could see the panic. What would happen if all the young ones left? Our group had been playful and fun-filled. The superiors were sensitive and discreet, business-like and friendly. They gave me money, but no letters of recommendation.

VII. It Has Been Said That a Religious Leaving Her Community Suffers a Trauma Comparable to That Endured by a Person Whose Spouse Has Died. Would You Agree with That Statement?

I agree that leaving the convent is a trauma comparable to the death of a spouse. I felt useless, unwanted, worth nothing, and like a number in a machine. I got a job through sheer luck, and have no complaints about opportunities, but I was miserable. I lived alone. There was no one to talk to. I went into debt. I went crazy buying books and clothing. I slept with a few men, one a priest. I began smoking and drinking.

It took me a long time to get over my guilt and the fear that I had let God down. I became so emotionally lost and in despair that I wanted to give up on life. I took a bottle of pills. My roommates came back unexpectedly and intervened.

I did not go through a trauma. The first year out of the convent was great. Everyone was helping me get started. By the second year I was on my own. I lived with two other women about my age, and we became close friends.

Leaving the convent is like a divorce. Death has a final separation that leaving the convent doesn't have. I did have some accidents, slight ones. (I do now when I am making a great change.) I didn't make erratic decisions. Making decisions was the hardest thing I had to learn. I didn't get into debt. I continued to do social work. I had a difficult time adjusting. I was not able to speak up about the impossible case load my boss gave me. I was asked to resign. I lived with members of my family for two years, but then lived alone. I needed the privacy. I had a male friend, but found out he was married. I was dumb in that regard. The second male friend was an alcoholic. I have good women friends. The third male friend is now my husband.

I can't agree with that statement. Losing a husband would be much more traumatic. I felt a sense of loss. I knew I had made the right decision, but I realized that my heart had to catch up with my mind. I missed the spiritual nourishment. I did not go into debt, get into accidents, or behave self-destructively. I got a job, and lived with my parents. My relationships with men and women were very good.

I never experienced a trauma, although I missed many of the nuns. I didn't make erratic decisions. I got a job soon after leaving the convent, and have never been without one since. I did not act self-destructively or go into debt. My relationships with people have been fairly normal, although I have felt hindered by hang-ups from convent life.

I could not say that leaving the convent caused me to suffer a trauma. I made no erratic decisions, nor did I get into accidents. Of all the nuns I have met who left, none has made erratic decisions. Nor has anyone found it traumatic. I did not get into debt. My immediate concern after leaving in 1966 was to get a job. I would say the greatest trauma for me was the stark reality of having no money, and having to survive. A Protestant seminary rector let me stay at the seminary for four dollars a day. He helped me get a job in a public school. I became a principal. When I reached sixty-five, I retired. I was ready to seek a quiet place.

I did not suffer as much trauma as I know some have. We had made many changes, and were in a short habit. I had stopped teaching, and was working in the inner city. For these reasons, I had an easier adjustment. I had a man interested in me, although I didn't get married. I had to learn about checking accounts and banking, how to buy clothes, and many other things. I wrote to and visited friends in the convent.

I agree with the statement. Investing twenty-five years with a community leaves one feeling lost when the ties are broken. I experienced a lot of stress. It took two years to overcome my depression.

I didn't suffer any trauma. The atmosphere of love and support that I lived in in my last few months in the convent helped me very much after I left. I became a social worker, working mainly with juvenile offenders.

———————

I agree with the statement. I did not get into accidents or into debt, but I increased my smoking from one to three packs a day, and I lost so much weight that I became anemic. I had a good job, but I worked ten to twelve hours a day because I didn't want to go back to my apartment. I was too lonely. I never cleaned my apartment, and I had no food in the refrigerator. I worked as a youth counselor. I started a sexual relationship with a man at work. It went on for five years. I made no women friends, but kept up with some of my friends from the convent.

———————

I felt no great trauma nor any physical or psychological effects. Sorry I cannot add more. Too busy.

———————

The trauma was terrible. The guilt was horrible. The adjustment was awful. I have never felt closer to losing my mind. I had no job, but was trying to finish up my master's degree. I was also preparing to get married. I was very depressed, and couldn't think. I was guilt-ridden over being happy about getting married. I gave up on the degree. It was too much. We got married, and moved into a rented house. I got a job teaching in an inner city school run by my old community. It was devastating. I lasted six weeks. It was the first time I had failed at anything.

———————

The pastor of my parents' parish had promised me a job, but the nuns at the school refused to have an ex-nun (even from another community) on the faculty. I borrowed $500 from a bank. I started graduate school, but couldn't stay with it. My mind was in a turmoil. I had terrible relationships with men, including old boy friends. I got pregnant, and had an illegal abortion. (It was 1967.) I got a job teaching third grade. I bought a car, but wrecked it within two months. I had never thought of doing anything except being a nun, and my social skills were pathetic. I wandered around in a daze for years.

––––––––––

Most of the trauma came from being a twenty-five year old woman with the social and emotional development of a teenager. I received support from my family, and things seemed to come my way when I needed them. I felt no guilt, and eventually the cord was cut.

––––––––––

When I left the convent, it was truly like a death for me. I didn't think it would bother me since I was so eager to leave. My last year in the community I had removed myself from the whole situation, but I still feel bitterness and resentment and sadness. I left because I believe in religious life, but not in the atmosphere of death and selfishness that existed in the convent.

––––––––––

When I left the community, it was the happiest day of my life. My first days out were spent buying clothes and looking for a job. I lived with another ex-nun.

––––––––––

I believe the community failed to meet its moral obligation to provide for the sisters who left. I had no social security or other pension credits after a lifetime of service. I did not get into debt, but I did have to buy things on credit because of the lack of capital. I had no unusual incidents. In fact, I felt as though I had never lived in the convent. There was no nostalgia, no regrets.

I felt so alone. I kept to myself. I dated a few men, but was not interested. I had too many other things on my mind. Psychotherapy was really the pits, although I am grateful for every minute of it.

I do agree with the statement. I never regretted my decision to leave, but I was lonely. My former sisters were supportive. I visited as needed, frequently in the beginning. Friends helped me learn basic survival skills. I felt the greatest disorientation in church. I had gone from leader to nobody. I found it hard to pray. I got into debt. It was hard to learn to manage money. I began to charge too much. I began to date again, but was turned off by men who thought I had either done it or was willing to.

I used to drive down to the convent at night. I'd drive past in my car. I'd drive to the school I taught in before leaving the convent, and look at it. I'd see some of my kids sometimes, but they wouldn't recognize me out of the habit. It was months before I stopped that.

No trauma, accidents or problems. I was naive about a number of things, especially working in a large organization. I was too trusting, probably too open and straight-forward. That was quickly corrected. I lived hand-to-mouth for six months while I finished my dissertation. Then I got a job teaching college. It was delightful.

I suffered severe trauma because I had identified so completely with the community. I got counseling, private and group, for a year.

I would agree with the statement. I found an excellent job. I also found a nice apartment. I lived in a town where friends from pre-convent days lived. Still I would have said then, and say now, that leaving my community was akin to having my right arm severed. It was extreme-ly painful. I began dating men from work, but found that I had little in common with them.

It was rough getting started. I lived with a charismatic family who helped me. They let me live with them rent free. I cared for the house and the kids. It was a healing time. I began to look for a job, but learned that my former community would not give me a recommendation.

Yes. Definitely yes. There were no support groups to go to when I left the convent in 1968. There were many people congratulating me on getting out, but few who understood the trauma at its depth. I have since been divorced, but my marriage was only to dull the pain of the greater separation.

It is worse. Losing a spouse leaves you with yourself, but leaving the convent involves you at the core. It leaves you wondering about your core's integrity. I made erratic decisions about men. I got into debt. My relationship with men was like that of a teenager.

VIII. Please Describe Your Life as It Is Now.

The man who is now my husband rescued me from the turmoil of the first years out of the convent. He helped me sexually, and financially.

I joined Reverend Moon's Unification Church sixteen months after I left the convent. I finished graduate school and my degree. I am married to a man chosen for me by Reverend Moon, a man also raised as a Catholic. I have no bitterness about the convent. I learned a great deal about myself and others there. I grew in many ways and learned to love God. I still have a deep hunger to live a life of love for God and humanity.

I am divorced. I walked out one Sunday after my husband was too demanding and inconsiderate about the heavy load I was carrying, my job and catering to his every need. I should never have gotten married. I do not intend to get married again. I have been relatively successful in my work. I am ready to begin something new.

It took me six or seven years to adjust. It was a process of learning, discovering, being prodded, being encouraged, hurting, healing, hurting, healing. I got married in 1976. My husband was fifty-four, and I was thirty-eight. The years since have proven our relationship. My personal life and my professional life are both important. We have no children, not at our ages.

I have been married for ten years. I have three children. It took me a year to bring my head and heart together. My family helped. It is only recently that I have learned to allow the deep sense within to unfold.

I never felt especially maladjusted. The gracious acceptance by my family was responsible for this. I did not really enjoy my first five years out of the convent. There were too many problems with the family I lived with. Eventually I bought a house and a small farm. I taught for several years, but have now taken a year off to work on a social justice program with some friends. I am not married. I am sixty years old. The most important thing in my life, more than ever before? God and the gospel of his son, Jesus.

The words of Hosea have become realized: "I will allure her into the desert, and in silence will speak to her heart." I have finally found what I set out to find at age sixteen. "I know Him in whom I believe." I experience story theology, community, liturgy, and love. I live alone most happily. I have loving relationships with friends. Any success I have I owe to my remarkable parents, after God, of course. I attribute none of it to convent life. For me, the miracle is that I was not more scarred by convent life. I am seventy-one.

I live with another woman, a teacher. I teach in a parochial school. My salary is low, but the job market is tight.
My friend and I share expenses. I enjoy teaching. I will
probably not marry. Statistics indicate that women
of forty-eight should get used to staying single. But
never say never is my motto.

I'm in no-man's land. I would like to become financially
independent and to share my life with someone. I am
living with my mother. I'm not married. I'm forty, and
want to go back to school. I don't feel I'm more or less
successful than other women who haven't experienced
convent life. Many women my age are finding themselves
and becoming independent whether it is because of
leaving the convent, divorce, or whatever.

It took me six years to adjust to the world outside,
and I am still growing. After five years of a wasteful
relationship, and spending all my time at work, I joined
several organizations and began to meet people. I became
involved in several activities, and met my husband.
We lived together for two years before we married.
We are happy. My marriage is the most important thing
in my life. Because of having been in the community,
I have an ideal personal and professional life. I learned
dedication and professionalism in the convent, and a
sense of community which helps in marriage. I am forty-
five. I have no children.

It has taken eight years to adjust. Sometimes I still
feel guilty about leaving. I am happily married and
the mother of two children. Our convent class is having
a twenty year reunion. I hope I have the guts to go.
I've been in therapy for six years. It has helped a great

deal. My family is the most important thing in my life and my own mental and physical health. My convent experience gave me many gifts, and enabled me to live the rich life I have today. My husband and I are a marriage encounter team, and love our ministry. I feel that my background has given me an advantage in experience and education over many people. I'm thirty-eight. I don't have any specific career goals, but I enjoy my wifely and motherly roles.

It took me five years to adjust fully to society. It was hard to stop thinking of myself as a stranger. I was naive enough to marry the first man I got involved with. We were married six years, and then divorced. He was a homosexual. This was my second traumatic split. However, we had a beautiful child, and I feel this was the reason we married. The traumas—the convent and the bad marriage—have strengthened me and made me a better person. I know what I want, and can understand other people. I am remarried. My husband is Jewish. I am very happy. I have stopped judging people by the Church's narrow standards, and begun to accept them for what they are. I am thirty-seven. The years without love have made me appreciate what love means.

I live with another former sister from my community. I am more dedicated to my work and have more expertise than others I work with. This causes difficulties. I am thirty years old, and still working through the death of leaving. I am doing much better now than I was a few months ago.

It took me about five seconds to adjust to the outside world. There were ten of us who left at the same time.

We were in our twenties and thirties, but we acted like young girls. We went to dances, gave parties, tried to meet men. I met my husband. We have three beautiful children. My husband was a member of an order of brothers. My marriage is a good one because I married late and had some sense. I am forty-eight. I have kept the wonderful friends I made in the convent.

I live alone. I am happy, and have good friends. I am considered successful. I am sixty-six. I hope to retire soon, but I have some reservations of a financial nature about the future.

I see religious life as ridiculous. The sisters I know are much better off than I am financially, and much more secure. They have the best of everything. They live in nicer places than I can afford. They have no worries about medical expenses or jobs. They take exotic vacations all over the place. I have lived a long time without a man and managed quite well. My freedom and independence have threatened some of them.

I am teaching, and working on a second master's degree. I am engaged to a wonderful, religious man. We are in a loving relationship, and hope to be married. I'm forty-one, and he is fifty. We do not plan to have children. I regret not marrying sooner, but don't feel it would be good to have children now.

Adjusting to the "world outside the convent" was barely perceptible. I never thought of myself as not in the world. I have been happily married for ten years, and have held a series of progressively more responsible jobs. I am forty-seven. It's difficult to compare my success with that of women who were not in the convent. In some ways my career would have progressed faster if I had not started so late. On the other hand, few women have doctorates or hold jobs paying $50,000 a year. Convent life was not a detriment to my career. On the contrary, in many ways I am grateful for the experiences of religious life.

I am relatively happy, but a restless spirit. I've been through heterosexual and homosexual romance in the past years. I'm not public about the fact that I'm gay.

I love my life now. Perhaps I could never have what I have now if the community had not loved and accepted me, and taught me how to live and give in all of life's situations. I married within a year of leaving. I met my husband in a soup kitchen. He was the director. He is bright, witty, Irish, deeply committed to Christian value and principles. I couldn't believe that such a man existed. We are deeply committed to the nuclear freeze movement. We are investigating the possibility of adopting a child from another country. I am thirty-two.

Since I left, I have gotten a master's degree in liturgy. I am thirty. I am comfortable being a single woman. I am looking for a husband.

My heart is still very much in the convent even though

I am married to a fine man. The vocation to religious life was so deeply burned into the core of my being that it can never be erased. Not all who left could say that. Some probably never missed it a day. But some of us were meant to be there, and the call just does not go away.

I am married and have two children. My husband is Jewish. We are living a typical middle-class life. It took about four to five years for me to adjust to life outside the convent. My equilibrium returned after I married. I am not sure if my convent experience con- tributed to my happiness today. I don't know if I would have had the same dedication. I am forty-nine.

IX. What Is Your Status in, or Your Opinion of, the Church of Today?

I wish the church would address the pressing problems of our world, poverty, hunger, oppressions, and the threat of nuclear war. Religion is important to me. I go to mass every weekend. I do spiritual reading daily. I often pray the liturgy of the hours. I am never mistaken for a nun. People can't believe I was in the convent. I still dream about the convent, and I am considering joining a third order. I have made several retreats. I am not in the least bit sorry that I spent a huge chunk of my life in the convent, nor do I regret one minute of it. It was in the providential scheme of things. I learned a tremendous amount about myself and other people. I am a more open and accepting person for having been in, and for having seen my own weaknesses both in and out. I don't judge people. I want to buy a piece of woods and hills. I am working on a book and on my business. I learned what poverty meant after I left the convent. I am not a follower. I am a leader, and I admire leaders.

I want to surrender to someone stronger than I am, a superior, a husband, a lover, God. If communities reached out in love and friendship to their former members, it would help everyone, those who left, the communities, the church, and even the world. The government does more for veterans than the convents did for their departed members. Their presumption that departing members had a warm and loving family waiting in the wings was unfounded and heartless.

The church is changing for the better in many parishes. I have never regretted being in the convent. It was a good experience, and channeled my life into disciplines that I would not have acquired otherwise. If I had it to do over again, I would turn around my career, and become a nun last—enjoying my retirement in contemplation and getting ready for heaven. If I were to found an order, it would be like the Peace Corps, three to five years in service to the church. No lifetime commitment. People would have their own apartments, and decide the course of their professional and personal life. The present superiors should shed their smugness, and address the problems of the poor, ill, and unfortunate. Like Mother Teresa, they should get out there and do the tough work instead of parading around in their immaculate convents.

I dreamed about the convent for six or seven years. I am a member of the Unitarian church now. I still meditate. It takes a different form, that of centering. People never believe that I was a nun. I am invited back to the convent, and I go. I am received warmly. If a girl asked me about entering the convent, I would ask her what she was running away from.

The church has missed the boat. The practices are artificial, and far removed from what is human. The message
of Christianity is lost. I almost never dream about the
convent anymore. I go back to visit, and am well received.
I think of my experiences in the convent with fondness.
It was a positive experience for me to live with so many
different people. The old nuns still in the convent are
living a model of religious life that died in 1970. They
are concerned with ritual and lip service. I would never
advise anyone to enter the convent. It is an escape
from reality. If I had it to do over again, I would do
it exactly the same way. There were things I needed
to learn in the convent, things about growing up. The
vows I took were a stumbling block to personal growth.
They seem meaningless today. The ideals of celibacy
and virginity are so wrong. If individuals want to choose
those things for themselves, fine. But no one should
make it mandatory. There is nothing Godlike in taking
away a person's humanity. Authority in the church
is misused and misguided. The clergy need to move
away from money and power. It's sad how many people
still want to be told what to do. We can fulfill God's
will by becoming functioning human beings.

In my parish I was an extraordinary minister, and a
parish council member, but they were just slots being
filled. I had no influence whatsoever. The church is
finally waking up to the role it can play in following
the gospel without compromise. I attend daily mass,
practice centering prayer, read scripture, attend charismatic meetings. I have been mistaken for a nun on several
occasions. I dream about the convent now and then.
My feelings about my old community are generally
good. They are putting the convent buildings to good
use, as day care centers for the elderly and retirement
homes. I often go back for visits, and am received gra-
ciously. I would encourage a young girl to enter the
convent. I'm not sorry I spent time in religious life.

I am a minister of the word, and have been asked to train the male eucharistic ministers. I love the church, and pray that all of us who are the church keep a listening heart to the spirit so we may be faithful to Him, the author of truth. I participate in daily mass. I tithe. I fast on Mondays. I pray the liturgy of the hours, meditate, and do spiritual reading every day. Many women I know do this. I am constantly inspired by the spirit working in the men and women I meet. In my dreams about the convent I am in, and trying to get out. I awake with relief and say thank God I am out. I feel sorry for my old community. I would never encourage a young girl to enter the convent. There is no need of communities. The communities feared or refused to face the truth. They were inbred, defensive, and they clung to structure above essence. They denigrated individuals, and failed to trust and affirm their members. They were not based on God's love. They distorted the evangelical counsels.

I am very involved in my parish. I believe priests should be allowed to marry. Women should be allowed to become priests. I am on the parish council, and am a member of several parish groups. I am a lector, and a distributor of communion. I am not in touch with my old community, but I am sure they are continually looking at new roles and updating old roles. I attended my twenty fifth reunion. I may return to the convent when my mother dies.

I still attend daily mass. I still wear the ring, although I had it slightly altered with some pearls. I am considered by many of the sisters to be one of them.

The church doesn't exist for me. I still dream about

the convent. I'm not sorry I spent time in religious life. Blind obedience can not replace responsibility to oneself.

I am in good standing with the church, and serve the church in many ways. I rejoice at the opening up of the church, but fear that the new is often embraced carelessly and at the expense of solid values and convictions. I am forty-six years old. I sometimes dream about the convent, but I no longer have nightmares about it. The community I was with is much diminished in numbers, and has a large number of old sisters to care for. They are worried, and unsure of what to do. They get one novice a year. I don't know what would attract anyone to such a life anymore. The community life is vestigial. The spiritual life is do-it-yourself. I still have many friends there. They had a reunion to which they invited former members. It was beautiful.

I am no longer a practicing Catholic. No aspect of religion is important except nostalgia. I don't dream anymore about the convent. I make decisions based on principles of community and dedication. I have been invited back by my community, and have gone. I am glad I spent time in the convent.

I'm angry at the church and disillusioned. I gave the best years of my life to the church, and I have no status because I am a woman. I was used. I will give it no more of my time or energy. I prefer serving where women are equals. I dream about the convent often. In my dreams I'm always leaving, and I don't know where to go. I feel a fondness for the old community. Through some of the sisters I came to love myself and see myself as valuable. I've never been invited back. I probably couldn't have handled going until now. I often reminisce with other ex-nuns about the old days.

I used to dream about nuns chasing me around. The time in the convent is very clear in my mind. Some spiritually sensitive persons have asked me if I was ever a nun.

I question the authority of the church. I attend services at a local parish and at a monastery where I feel similar values. There are members of my old community who speak to me now who never spoke to me while I was in the community. Suddenly everyone is friendly. I would discourage a young woman from entering the convent. The life is artificial. I have thought about entering a different order, but I have been very wounded, and am not sure that I would find anything different from what I have already experienced. I feel cheated that I cannot live in a community. I was called to such a life, but the self-centeredness and worldly values made it impossible to stay. I miss the religious experience and personal growth workshops. Once you have known more, you cannot settle for less.

I am not too involved with the church. I get my children to mass on Sunday if nothing else is happening. The community I was in has very few members left. They live in apartments. They should sell the buildings and use the money to feed the poor. I have been back to reunions. It was great seeing everyone again. I would not advise anyone to enter. My biggest fear is that my daughter would want to. I am a feminist, and will never return to religious life. I do not believe that anyone should take final vows. We all change.

My status today is that of a laywoman in the church: you know what that status is. I am a reader at our parish. We have an active and interesting program. I am at home there. The liturgy is beautifully done, and strikes a chord. I have little contact with my former community. Many have left, and few are entering. Things that were considered radical when I suggested them are commonplace now. How soon will the communities disappear? I'm not a sociologist. I don't know. I am grateful for the good things I received from the community. I remember it with affection. I wish I had not wasted so many years of my life. I would have been happy married. I get lonesome at times. I have a great family, but each one has his or her interests, and I always return home alone. I see no reason why a woman should not be ordained. I resent the lack of true acceptance of women by priests.

I'm not sorry I spent time in religious life. I'm just sorry it didn't work out for me. My biggest mistake was expecting my community to live up to what they claimed were their ideals. I was not tolerant of failures, least of all my own. I couldn't understand how we could call ourselves religious and not have time for prayer, or poor and never know want, or chaste while being unloving.

I'm still searching for a place in the church. I attend mass and observe most rules. I do not accept the church's teaching on birth control. It is a matter for each couple to decide. I dream about the convent, usually about going back. I am grateful for my years in the convent. I grew emotionally and spiritually. If someone asked me about entering, I would say go and see. It's well worth the effort.

I attend mass from time to time, but am embarrassed by the irrelevant homilies preached by a clergy that is out of touch with today's problems. My husband is against religious activism of any kind, but if I felt strongly about involvement, I'd risk his displeasure. The community I belonged to is aging fast. They are selling property. They choose their own work now. I have been invited back several times, and when I went, I was treated as an integral part of the community. I see little point in women living a religious life. It is far more important for women to be leaders in issues of importance than to try to fit outmoded forms of behavior. I do not regret the years I spent in religious life. I was saved from the life many of my peers pursued in the 1950s—early marriage, several kids, meager education, dead-end jobs.

When I read about church matters, I am amazed that people still take it seriously. When that nun was kicked out of her order in Michigan, I thought all the others would walk out with her, hand in hand, and leave the male hierarchs holding the empty building. But no. They twittered for a few days, and then acceded to the pope's judgment of their sister. Anything rather than jeopardize their security. The American orders were founded to be little harems for the bishops and priests, and the old harem girls continue their loyal service. So what if one is pushed out if her activities displease her male masters? How can people believe the Creator wants them to turn their backs on her good gifts? Why would she want them to neglect the talents their ancestors bequeathed them? We will all rest in her gardens some day, and watch the movies of each other's lives. We will understand why our biological urge to follow leaders allowed us to be led by some of the most messed-up men who ever lived—men who think of women as occasions of sin, unclean, and subhuman.

I am a part of a loose network of committed Christians. The American bishops are increasingly aware of real-life issues, and are meeting them with faith. Small segments of the laity are reading the documents, and thirsting for knowledge. I'm a typical N.C.R. reader, liberal, liturgical, educated, peripheral in the church. I consider myself a Catholic, but am pained by the way individuals get screwed by the rules. The mystery of the worshipping community is distorted by the silly rules, the personalities, and politics. I love our church, and sometimes hate it. I choose to belong, blood and bones, forever. I'm glad for all my experiences, and wish others as much good.

We are denied the true history of our church. The priests speak from the pulpit, but not of the earliest days when women were equal. Jesus was married, but we never hear of his wife. We are taught to honor saints who were just names superimposed over older names of pagan gods and goddesses. We are taught to take literally bits of scripture that scholars (and most ordinary clergy) know are the products of a society which considers women property. Thou shalt not covet thy neighbor's wife. Nor his other stuff. Would Jesus guess what was going on if he walked into mass? Why do men take a real thing—a meal—and distort it with ritual until it becomes unrecognizable? Why don't women stop cooperating with their rituals, and do something real? Something Jesus and his friends, female and male, did—enjoy a meal together? A meal calls for real food, wine, and conversation. Women don't need to be ordained by male bishops. We are capable now, and always have been, of serving true and nourishing food, and giving real love. That is communion.

My husband and I attend Mass, read and discuss U.S.
Catholic and N.C.R., and are involved in the Catholic
Worker movement. I dream about the convent. There
are things I miss very much. I sacrificed camaraderie
for intimacy. My old community is small now. They
will probably not exist in fifty years. I think the thousands
who entered in the early 1960s were victims of the
times. There was wholesale discrimination against women,
and they saw religious life as a way to contribute to
society and escape pushing a baby carriage in the suburbs.
With the confusion of the post-Vatican II era, they opted
out. I am not sorry I spent time in religious life. I resent
the position of women in the church. I am in favor of
the ordination of women and of optional celibacy. I
am opposed to the Church's teaching on birth control.
It has often crossed my mind that should I become a
widow, there would be no reason why I wouldn't consider
a return to religious life.

If I cannot find a community to get into, I'll have to
found one. I recently got a degree that would enable
me to work more freely in the church, but the opportunity
is not that great for a woman. If I had my life to live
over, I would choose a contemplative order. I have trouble
with the authority of the church. I listen, sift, disregard,
and make up my own mind. God is greater than the
men who run the show.

The motherhouses and juniorates are empty. They would
make good minimum security prisons.

X. Comments by Women Still in Religious Life.

I stay because I choose to, and because in some lovely
moments I know that I may have changed, but the Lord
does not. This gives me some measure of stability and
trust. I am generally well-liked, but there are some
who do not like me, company people and sisters who
function in cliques. They are puzzled by me because
I do not hesitate to write letters to newspapers on important issues. I express my opinions in the community
even when they are not the opinions of the majority.
I have been elected a number of times to the policy
making council of our community. Recently, however,
I lost an election. I felt it would be my last hurrah for
the congregation. I am well-known in the diocese, and
have connections that might have helped us. I wish
I felt more at home in the community than I do. I am
relaxed and at home with several, but not with all.
I am viewed as a threat by some, by others as bright,
hard-working, energetic, involved, imprudent at times,
articulate, warm, kind, compassionate, impulsive, talka-
tive, well-groomed, socially and politically concerned.

Half of our community left, those younger than I and
those up to ten years older. Our median age is sixty
plus. We've had to cut back services and rethink what
we will do about retirement. Sometimes we have too
much concern for money, but we always have good
women who call us back to vision rather than utility.
Many good sisters left, and many stayed. Some not
so good have stayed, and have caused problems for
themselves and others. I have considered leaving, but
it seems that here is where I belong. I'm lucky enough
to have friends and a spiritual director who have encouraged me to look long and hard at who I am.

Seven or eight percent of our community left. It hurt to see them leave. They were very dear, but rebellious or insecure. Their leaving caused me to question my self, my life, my value to the church. Some gifted people left. Many had personal problems, and still do, but some were good religious, and all were valuable people. I thought about leaving, but had no desire to break my commitment with the Lord. I'm very happy, and have friends in my community and in the parishes where I've worked. When I get old, my community will care for me in our infirmary. We have invited our former members back to visit. We feel free to visit them.

Ten percent of our community left. A few sisters were shaken by the exodus, but myself, no. I felt and still feel very strongly about my vocation and my life commitment. I did not ever consider leaving. I intend to remain in my community. I love it, and am very happy. I have good friends in the community. My community will care for me in old age just as we care for each other now, and for the elders. I understand the vows more clearly now than at the time of my profession. Therefore, they mean more to me. Most of our former members left with no ill feelings toward us. They return for friendly visits, and all know they are most welcome. I intend to continue striving to fulfill and live up to the spirit of our founder by living the gospel of Jesus Christ. We have a relaxed spirit, and much freedom to live our own lives. I am at home in my community. I do not have power because I do not exert my power. I am an extreme introvert, and find that asserting myself is difficult. This is not a fault of my community. We have one novice and one postulant. We share the manual work. We have hired men and women to do the heavy work. I would have the women seeking entrance be older, more mature. If someone asked me, I would let her see what community life means to me. I would encourage her to enter our order. Others, no.

One seventh of our community left. This caused much anxiety and guilt among the nuns who stayed. I don't feel the best left, but some very promising members did leave. Some of them were the visionaries and the creative people. It never occurred to me to leave. The conflicts they suffered never hit me. I'm not saying that any of us were spared the pain. Many of our close friends left, and that was hard. I am the superior of our community. I am very happy with our growth. I have many friends. For me, relationships are the cement of community life. I have little concern about old age. The community has made provision as far as is humanly possible, and the rest I leave to God. Few of our members left in bitterness. We have invited them back. We try to keep their addresses up to date. My goals are to be open to the new trends and challenges for religious. There is constant new interpretation for our life and vows. Our median age is fifty-six. There has been a complete shift of apostolates. We have left the classrooms to do parish ministry, religious education, and diocesan level work. I am in my second term as superior. I feel at home in the community. I'd like to help some individuals who are finding the new trends hard to accept. They suffer, and cannot relax with the Spirit. I am seen as gentle, level-headed, and middle-of-the-road. Many consider me more spiritual than I feel. If I could re-live the influx before 1965, I'd suggest more screening. The exodus could have been handled in a more healing manner. The community needed more help in accepting diversity. When young women come today, I try to be honest with them. We are still shifting through changes. New members are welcome to bring their gifts to the struggle.

One third of our community left. A deep sadness gripped our hearts to see them leave the life of dedication they had vowed to God. Their departure created a fissure in the integrity of the community. Their work had to be assumed by others. Most of those who left were good sisters until a short time before they left. Some fell into some vice such as falling in love with a man

or building up a craving to have a family of their own.
The question of leaving flashed through my mind, but
I remembered that I had vowed my life to God, and
he expected me to keep my promise. I am a retired
teacher. I work with senior citizens. God has been good
to me. I have friends in the community, mostly sisters
who entered when I did. I will be cared for in the infirmary when I am old. Our superior sends Christmas cards
to former members of the community. Once we invited
them back. So far, no retreat has been scheduled for
them. We show them every kindness when they visit.
Personally, I would have adhered to the original interpretation of the vows given me during my novitiate.
My superiors have given me a new interpretation today.
I accept it, and offer it to God as my way of fulfilling
the vows once made to him. I hope we use all the talents
and material goods God has given us to further his king-
dom on earth. I have some power in our community.
I am consulted by my sisters in areas in which I have
some skill. I would like to see more silence in the convent
and a return to more simple living, for instance in the
wardrobe of some sisters. There should have been closer
screening of those who entered before 1965. A competent
spiritual director might have been able to save some
vocations. Trusted friends could have helped some of
the sisters stay in the convent.

I will be cared for in old age by my sisters. I helped
put on a homecoming for former members. Our median
age is sixty plus. I no longer have the official position
in which I served for many years, but serve on committees.
I am respected and loved. We should have scrutinized
those who entered before 1965 more closely. I don't
know what we should have done about departures. I
would encourage a young woman to enter religious life.

Thirty percent of our community left. The wound was
long in healing. Some of the best chose to leave. It

caused us to re-evaluate our lives. I have never considered leaving. I will remain here for the rest of my life. My work is fulfilling and rewarding, and makes me happy. My vibrant, prayerful, visionary community makes me happy also. I will be cared for here at the motherhouse in old age. We have had several get-togethers with former members. We receive them with joy and gratitude. I intend to continue participating in community building. I am an officer. I intend to extend my own spiritual development through prayer, liturgy, and private reflection. At the time of my profession, my interpretation of the vows was rather negative. Now I see them as positive and growth-inspiring. Poverty frees me to live simply. Chastity frees me to love my Lord Jesus with my whole heart and soul. Obedience is a real collaboration with my superior to plan my life strategy. She helps me discern how I can best serve my God, my community, my self. Our median age is sixty. Our goal is to recruit new members to keep alive our charism, and to witness to the surrounding community and to the church at large that religious life is as valid now as it always was. I have power in my community, and I feel very much at home. I am seen as happy, as one who works hard and plays hard, as a peacemaker, a sensitive listener, full of energy, enthusiastic, and one who accepts responsibility. If we had changed faster, many of our prophets and visionaries would have stayed. I would encourage a young woman to enter the convent. We have so many blessings such as the opportunity for common prayer, space for private prayer, the possibility to serve God's special ones and to witness the gospel.

My community is middle-of-the-road, liberal with the brakes on, like the country. There is enough openness for liberals to survive. I am seen as very intelligent and verbal. I am accepted for my brains, even sought after, but I am not at the middle of things. I'm not a submissive member of the community. I'm critical, but loyal. Sometimes I feel that I am being tolerated. To someone who wanted to enter, I would say, it's a

good place if it's for you. Know yourself, and be true
to yourself, and give it a go.

The spirit of our community is warm, loving, supportive,
prayerful, dedicated. Our novices are being prepared
to understand the church and religious life of the future.
I am happy, warm, personable, trusting, honest, and
religious. When young girls ask me about religious life,
I tell them I have found great joy and peace, but it
has not been easy. I've had opportunities for education,
spiritual growth, but it depended on me to use the opportunities. There are hard times in every life because
we are human. The blessings, friendships, and opportunities of religious life can't be equalled in any other calling.

One third of our community left, including my two
best friends. Many who left should have gone sooner,
but the climate on the outside was too hostile, and
they hesitated. Others had entered for the wrong reasons,
to wear a habit, or to be respected as a special person.
I considered leaving, but in my heart I knew I would
regret it. I had a dream that I had left. When I awakened,
I was happy that it was only a dream. It served as a
warning that, in spite of all my inner anger, I could
never be happy elsewhere. I have not missed having
children, but I have missed not having a husband. In
the convent I am not really special to any one person,
and that is hard. We are well cared for in old age. We
have had reunions with former members. I went to the
first one. We are just not on the same wave length.
I live alone near the motherhouse. This is accepted.
I have lived in convents where sisters spent their time
in their rooms and hardly ever participated in community
activities. My life now has helped me discover my inner
resources, my sincerity, and the joy of having my own
place to reflect my personality and taste. I know I will
live with a group again. I will have to if I live to be

old and decrepit. So be it. Since the discipline in our
community was so strict, the pendulum swung for awhile
to the other extreme. It took time for some of the nuns
to learn to dress in a manner befitting middle-aged
professional women. Many conservative clergymen
think we have gone to the dogs, but I am proud that
our community espouses worthwhile causes. I think
members of the community in power are too political.
I wonder if they have the future good of the community
at heart or personal ambition. I can understand their
mentality since we were squelched in our youth. We
are at a critical crossroads. Our median age is over
sixty.

Part Two: The Communities

It was 1790 when the first convent was established in the United States. Before that, colonial women who wanted to become nuns entered communities in Canada, Europe and New Orleans. The nuns who founded the first convent in the United States were three Americans and an Englishwoman from the Carmel of Hoogstraeten, Belgium. In 1790, they settled on 800 acres in Maryland: their first novice, Elizabeth Carberry of St. Mary's County, entered the following year. Like every community to follow, the Carmelites had to earn a living; there would be no endowments and no royal patrons in America. Bishop John Carroll urged them to obey a directive from Rome and become teachers, but they refused, preferring to spin wool and bind books. They put their slaves to work raising sheep. Nearly every community which survived this early period owed its success to slave labor: novices brought enslaved servants to convents as part of their dowries, and benefactors, perhaps through guilt, bequeathed slaves to convents in their wills. Like most slaveholders, the Carmelites had problems with overseers. They had another problem as well, one which would plague other religious communities down to the present—lawsuits. By 1831 it had all become too much: the Carmelites sold their thirty slaves, and moved to Baltimore to open a school. They had observed the success other communities were having with their select schools and academies.[1]

The Academy of the Visitation, begun in poverty thirty years earlier, had by this time one hundred pupils in the select school—enough to support one hundred fifty students in the free school and fifty seven nuns.[2]

In the Carmelites' history, it is said that the slaves were allowed to choose their new owners. In the history

of the Ursulines of New Orleans, it is said that slaves
were instructed in the faith, and allowed to marry in
the sisters' chapel.[3]

In 1798 three women of Irish birth became the
first American Visitandines. Their academy in George-
town, taken over from a community of French Poor
Clares who had given up and returned home, was a success
from the start. The capitol moved to Washington in
1800, and diplomats from Catholic countries sent their
daughters to the Visitation. Rich American Protestants,
following the example of Thomas Jefferson whose daughter had studied at a fashionable convent in Paris, began
entrusting their children to the nuns as well.

Bishops and priests were deeply concerned with
nuns' wearing apparel. Bishop Neale, founder of the
Visitandines, was typical. Before 1815, "the sisters
wore a quasi-conventual dress, which he had several
times modified without satisfaction. The long black
veil and habit, the barbette and silver cross were wanting.
At length he determined to let them wear the Teresian
costume, and wrote to his brother Charles at Port Tobac-
co to send him a model of it, from the convent there.
'A large doll, fully equipped, was immediately forwarded;
and the bishop, calling together Mother Teresa and
such of the sisters as were most dexterous with the
needle, had the dimensions taken, and habit, the gimp,
etc., cut out in his presence.'"[4]

Saint Elizabeth Seton founded the Sisters of Charity
in 1809. St. Joseph's Academy, like the Visitation, suc-
ceeded in attracting paying students. At first the sisters
supplemented their income by sewing for college boys,
but soon their select school was supporting them and
their free school. Bishop Carroll wanted them to raise
their social status by affiliating with the French Daughters of Charity—the cornette sisters, but Mother Seton
refused; she disliked the idea of turning over the direction
of her band of friends and relatives to a foreign superior,
and she knew American sisters had to accept paying
students or starve. The reputation of the Sisters of
Charity spread quickly: in 1814 they were given charge
of an orphanage, and in the 1820s they were given hospitals in Baltimore and St. Louis.

In Kentucky in 1812, a Belgian priest, Charles

Nerinckx, founded the Sisters of Loretto. Their first superior, Mary Rhodes, sold a slave to finance the venture. The rule Nerinckx gave the nuns was so bizarre —"revolting," Bishop Benedict Flaget of Bardstown called it—that following his death it was modified; the deaths of several young nuns who had contracted tuberculosis precipitated the changes. Nerinckx had required the nuns to go barefoot, to sleep in their clothes, and to dig a grave with their hands for the next to die. He forbade them to teach grammar, a subject he considered too frivolous for the children of Kentucky. He kept the widows and virgins apart: the blacks were to be kept as perpetual postulants. The sisters' second director, Guy Chabrat, sent the blacks home, and required the nuns to turn in Nerinckx's writings to be burned.[5]

A French priest, John David, founded a community of Sisters of Charity in Kentucky in 1812. Their first superior, Elizabeth Wells, transferred to another order, but under the second superior, Mother Catherine Spaulding, the order flourished. David gave them a rule similar to that observed by the French Daughters. He refused to unite his nuns with Mother Seton's community, preferring to retain control himself. The Kentucky sisters, like those in Maryland, relied on slave labor and tuition fees from their students for their livelihood.[6]

A Dominican, Samuel Wilson, founded a community of Dominican sisters in Kentucky in 1822. He gave them a rule which required them to do the work of active sisters and observe the prayer schedule of cloistered nuns: besides teaching, farming, carpentry, and spinning and weaving, the sisters rose for midnight prayer.

The Oblates of Providence, the first community of black sisters, began in Baltimore in 1829. They were often without the sacraments; racial prejudice prevented chaplains from ministering to them.

In the 1820s, Richard Miles, the first director of the Dominicans of St. Mary's of the Springs, permitted the nuns to contract a $2000 debt. When he was transferred, the second chaplain, Rafello Munos, ordered the religious to sell their convent to pay off the debt, and then disband and return to their parents' homes. When they refused, he withdrew the Blessed Sacrament.[7]

In 1823 two brothers of Samuel F.B. Morse began publishing "The New York Observer," the newspaper which would dominate the anti-Catholic press: in 1826 Charles G. Finney began the revivalist movement. The renewed intolerance and religious excitement were in reaction to the liberal deism of the early post-revolutionary period. Catholics, tolerated at that earlier time, now became the targets of oppression once again. The trustee controversy, the papal jubilee, the Baltimore Provincial Congress, and the growth of foreign immigration all fueled the fires of hatred. In 1829 the Catholic Emancipation Act in England unleashed a flood of violence in England and the United States. The anti-Catholic papers featured convent tales from the start.[8]

In 1831, when the Carmelites opened their school, and when the most difficult period in the history of American nuns was about to begin, certain patterns already were set. Already nuns were relying on tuition payments from non-Catholics: in some select schools as many as two thirds of the students were Protestant or Jewish. In an advertisement, the Carmelites assured the citizens of Baltimore that pupils of all denominations would be accepted with no interference with their religious principles. The mobs of working class fundamentalists who burned convents in this period were attacking not only nuns, but their students as well—the daughters of Unitarians and other liberal Protestants. Already peculiar rules were being written, and regulations, works, and devotional practices were multiplying; priests, trained in the Jansenist seminaries of Europe, were imposing schedules on nuns which would kill them. Tuberculosis, the killer of overworked young nuns, had claimed its first victims. Already priests were fussing over nuns' habits, and using the eucharist as a weapon. The threat to withdraw the sacraments pulled many a group of nuns over to a priest's point of view.

Not every nun was utterly passive. When Abbot Boniface Wimmer commanded Mother Evangelista Kremmeter to expel Mother Benedicta Riepp for disagreeing with him, she refused. "How could I treat my own sisters thus? If your orders must be complied with, I will feel constrained to leave and to secure salvation in a stricter order."[9]

Leaving was easy in those days. Mary McNulty was a Sister of Charity in 1829. She left to join the B.V.M. community in Iowa. She returned to the Sisters of Charity, then became a founding member of a group of Dominicans. Finally she became an Ursuline in New Orleans.[10]

The priest who ruled the Sisters of Charity of Dubuque, Iowa, Terence J. Donaghoe, became too sick to say Mass, but refused to allow the nuns to call in another priest; he feared "meddling," and the sisters "did not like to bother him."[11] They expelled two of their sisters for complaining about not receiving the sacraments even on Sunday. Donaghoe held all the community's goods in his own name, including the nuns' patrimonies, but refused to make a will. Finally, the nuns called in the bishop who forced the dying priest to sign a will. Donaghoe then turned to one of the nuns and said, "This is your work. It is just like you."[12]

Money frequently was an issue between communities of women and their male superiors. Abbot Boniface Wimmer, given a large sum of money by German donors for the Benedictine sisters under his direction, decided to keep it for himself.[13]

It was difficult for women to survive without male protection in nineteenth-century America. It was particularly difficult for nuns to survive in a cultural setting where they were considered dangerous, unlucky, and of questionable morality. They had to rely on priests. Many of the clergymen of this era, Frenchmen and Irishmen, Spaniards and Italians, came to this country to escape problems in Europe. There were drunkards and eccentrics among them. Some were running from anti-clericalism. Many had been suspended in the old country, but convinced the American bishops to give them emergency faculties. The time lag in getting mail from Europe enabled unfit priests to establish themselves.

In this age of oratory and religious enthusiasm, debates between Catholic priests and Protestant ministers were a popular form of entertainment: after 1835 ex-nun shows became the rage. Maria Monk, Josephine Bunkley, Rebecca Reed, and many others traveled the revival circuit with their male promoters horrifying their audiences with tales of convent life.

The hatred Americans felt for nuns came from various sources. Some associated nuns with freemasonry; the Ursulines of Nantes had made George Washington's masonic apron. Others despised nuns because they believed the select schools existed to provide converts for Rome.

Books about ex-nuns were the pornography of the nineteenth century: they told of sex between nuns and priests, underground passageways, murdered babies, whips, chains, midnight escapes, everything a fevered imagination could desire. They found an immediate audience; it was a respectable way of getting something sexy to read. After the events of the 1830s, book publishers, organizers of lecture tours, and propaganda agents began cooperating in the first media blitz. There was money to be made: ministers grew rich and famous with anti-Catholic lecture tours. Publishers began selling books in numbers unimagined before.

In 1834 a mob of brickmakers and other working class fundamentalists burned the Ursuline convent at Charlestown, Massachusetts, a school attended by Catholic girls and by the daughters of Unitarians. This event was precipitated by a dispute between the town selectmen and Bishop Fenwick over a graveyard on Bunker Hill, by tales told by a dismissed candidate, Rebecca Reed, by the behavior of a troubled religious—Elizabeth Harrison—who left the convent one night and returned the next day, and by the sermons of Lyman Beecher. On the night of August 11, the convent was put to the torch. The nuns and the students, the town selectmen and the firemen watched.[14] After the riot, Rebecca Reed's book, **Six Months in a Convent**, was published. It was an immediate success. It prepared the way for the enduring classic of the genre, **The Awful Disclosures of the Hotel Dieu Nunnery of Montreal.** This book was published in 1836 by Harper Brothers, who set up a dummy company in the names of two employees, Howe and Bates. They sold 300,000 copies of the book before 1860.[15]

Maria Monk, said by her mother to be brain-damaged, had lived at the Hotel Dieu for a short time but had never been a nun. That fact did not deter Harper Brothers or the Protestant clergymen who wrote the book and exploited her for their gain. Maria Monk's success spawned an industry. The superiors reviled in the ex-nun books wrote their own books, and allowed delegations to come in and search their convents. Maria Monk's mother wrote a book. Her daughter wrote a book. The delegations wrote books.

The environment of fear created at this time had much to do with the way Catholics would regard ex-nuns down through the decades: the communities' unjust treatment of their former members in modern times may be traced back to this period, and understood in the light of torch-bearing mobs.

The image of nuns was modified somewhat in those cities where the only women willing to help victims of the cholera epidemics were religious.

The barrage of anti-Catholic literature continued. Harry Hazel's **The Nun of St. Ursula** was a best seller in the 1840s.

It is said that the poorest cabin on the frontier possessed two books: the Bible and Maria Monk.

This was a time of growth for women's communities; hunger and political unrest were driving Irish and German families from their homes. New religious communities were formed to serve the immigrants, and older congregations began to change. Mother Seton was dead now, and the Sisters of Charity split apart. One group affiliated with the French Daughters of Charity, a move Mother Seton had opposed. They adopted the cornette, and gave their orphanages to Sisters of Mercy and Sisters of St. Joseph; the Jansenist-tainted French rule forbade them to teach boys or to change the diapers of male babies. The other groups, which became the Sisters of Charity of New York and of Cincinnati, retained the cap and Mother Seton's rule.

Some women's orders, instead of breaking apart, attempted to become more firmly united: they were prevented from doing so by bishops who wanted absolute control over the religious in their dioceses. In 1847 the Sisters of St. Joseph tried to form a central government, but bishops refused to let nuns from their various dioceses attend the meeting. The suspicion and fear with which one community would come to regard another, even of the same order, were fostered by bishops.

During the Mexican War, nuns supplemented their income by sewing shot bags for the army at a penny apiece.

Escaped nuns continued to be popular attractions on the revival circuit: in the 1840s, escaped Mormons could be heard as well.

Many nuns came from Europe in the 1840s. Some communities sent out groups to find postulants or to raise money in the United States: these religious found work here among the Catholic immigrants, and never returned to the old cloisters. Other European houses sent nuns in response to the requests of bishops or priests who asked for teachers for their new parochial schools: the textbooks used in public schools, filled with anti-Catholic propaganda as they were, made Catholic schools necessary. In New York alone, fifty-six new secondary schools for girls began at this time. Nuns staffed hospitals, homes for working girls, orphanages, homes for the aged, and homes for "wayward" girls.

In the 1850s, communities split. The boy question which had troubled the Sisters of Charity was a problem for other communities as well; if their constitutions specified the education of girls, the nuns felt they must obey. Bishops continued to break communities of women apart: they wanted nuns who were fully submissive, and not under the direction of a mother superior in another diocese. They moved individual sisters around from mission to mission, forced some others to disband, forced founders to leave their communities, opened and closed schools without consulting the nuns who staffed them, and wrote to Rome to block the approval of constitutions which failed to give them absolute power.[16]

Bishop Peter Lefevere sent a letter to the superior of the Immaculate Heart of Mary Sisters informing her that he had appointed a priest—a foreigner and a stranger—to take over from her the direction of her community.[17] She went to live with the Grey Nuns in Canada, and the sisters of her community were forbidden to write to her for eighteen years. Saint John Neumann of Philadelphia was involved in the split of this community. A priest in Nashville split a group of Sisters of Charity of Nazareth, Kentucky from their community so they could sing in his choir. Later, he left the diocese and Bishop Richard Miles who had left the Dominican sisters in a similar situation earlier in his life, refused to pay the debt on the convent which had been built with his permission. Without his protection, the nuns could not survive; Mother Xavier Ross went to St. Louis to ask Bishop Kenrick to permit her sisters to settle in his diocese. He refused. Pierre de Smet suggested she talk to John Miege, Vicar Apostolic of Indian Territory, Kansas: Miege permitted the Sisters of Charity to come to Leavenworth.[18] The delicacy with which the convent historians treated the old bishops is remarkable: in this instance, Bishop Miles is forgiven because of the difficulties of his early missionary activities.

The hatred of Catholics and the violence against nuns continued. The Sisters of Mercy of Providence, Rhode Island were attacked by Yale students: Yale and Harvard men were deeply involved in nativist activities. Mobs continued to burn convents and orphanages, to poison nuns' wells, and to force the closing of schools for black children.

The German communities required the Americans who entered to learn German, to pray and teach in German, and to live by schedules established in medieval times for cloistered nuns: this would have consequences in the 1890s. The attempts European nuns made to observe enclosure in their raw new convents made them appear ridiculous. Some watched their students from a window at recess rather than break cloister by stepping outside. One group "went without heat for a day and a night before aid came. Automatic excommunication would have been incurred by a sister who stepped outside to replenish the supply of wood."[19] Some nuns wore face veils in public, and spoke to guests through grilles. Abbot Boniface Wimmer refused to give the Benedictine sisters of Minnesota a chaplain, thus forcing them to leave the cloister to go to mass.[20]

Nuns were concerned with social status. The communities continued to differentiate between lay and choir sisters: the fraus wore a train on their habit, for instance, while the schwesters wore a simpler garb. Mother Seton's sisters who disobeyed her wishes and joined with the French Daughters of Charity did so in part to attain a more elevated standing in the church. The histories of many communities contain lists of rich families whose daughters attended their academies.[21]

The traditional obligation of the choir nun, the Divine Office, was taken away at this time: in the 1850s, the bishops, observing the fact that sisters were overworked, took the Divine Office from most communities, and replaced it with the Little Office of the Blessed Virgin Mary. Without the Divine Office and enclosure, the women in the American communities were of questionable canonical status. The men who ruled convents could disestablish them if the sisters disobeyed.

Most nuns submitted with varying degrees of docility to the men who ruled them: those who did not found little understanding from other women: when Mother Benedicta Riepp, one of the boldest nuns of the nineteenth century, returned to her motherhouse in Germany for clarification about who was to rule her community, Abbot Wimmer or the bishops or the superiors in Germany, she was treated with suspicion, and kept isolated from the community.[22]

The image of nuns began to change ever so slightly in the 1850s: a more romantic view was emerging from the Oxford movement, and some Americans were impressed by the charity with which nuns cared for children left homeless by the cholera epidemics of 1849 and 1854. But for many Protestant Americans, the old ideas were still potent: the Know-Nothing movement, the visit of Cardinal Bedini, and a new crop of escaped nun books renewed the attacks on convents. The best seller of 1854, Charles W. Frothingham's **Six Hours in a Convent,** sold 40,000 copies in one week.

The Sisters of St. Francis of Assisi of Milwaukee were made into servants of a seminary. They had to take turns living their rule: they described themselves as "crucified by their work." The seminarians complained about their cooking. The priests who directed them required them to work without pay because of the debt on their house. The superiors were forced to withdraw: they became priests' housekeepers and church janitors. "They were models of the retired life they had wished to live and could not."[23]

In the 1860s the image of American nuns changed. Religious communities sent bands of nuns to nurse in army hospitals: hundreds of nuns volunteered to travel to the front. Wounded soldiers whose previous knowledge of nuns had come from the anti-Catholic press now came to love their gentle nurses. The various communities' histories record the adventures and courageous deeds of their nuns of the 1860s. Mother Teresa Maher, for example, a Sister of Mercy of Cincinnati, is remembered for searching the battlefield at Shiloh in the night with a lantern, raising each head, looking in each face to make sure no living man had been left with the dead.[24] The Sisters of the Holy Cross from Notre Dame dug wounded men from frozen mud to carry them to shelter.[25] Dorothea Dix tried to prevent sisters from nursing in army hospitals: the hundreds who did so reported directly to the various commanders. A monument in Washington, D.C. commemorates their services.

The communities established a reputation for excellence in nursing at this time which would survive for a generation. The nuns who served in the Civil War never forgot their experiences. For years after the war, the Sisters of the Holy Cross, on the night before they left for their missions, gathered to sing the old song, "Tenting Tonight." The angel of the battlefield shielding a wounded prisoner of war from would-be executioners with her own body, or writing a last letter for a dying boy, enclosing a lock of his hair, whispering an act of contrition in his ear, was a powerful new image.[26]

In the decade following the Civil War, thousands of orphaned children were placed in the care of nuns. The bishops were anxious not to offend the Protestant majority: they were afraid sisters might try to proselytize non-Catholic children in their care. It was necessary to stiffen control. The bishops wrote letters to Rome asking for clarification of the role of the women's communities, questioning their rules, their garb, their behavior, the validity of their vows, and their canonical status. Some bishops, dissatisfied with the orders, established new ones which would accept direction more readily.

Bishops continued to split communities apart, and to throw out election results which displeased them.

Nuns were at the mercy of the bishops. Nuns who had
seen the convents burn and heard the mobs were still
alive; the old fears and the training in obedience were
too strong. Without espiscopal protection, nuns could
not attract students to their schools: without tuition
fees they would starve. Whatever the bishops chose
to bind on earth, nuns and all Catholics believed, however
whimsical it might appear, or absurd or unjust or unchrist-
like, was bound in heaven.

The Sisters of the Precious Blood were ordered
by Bishop Baltes of Alton, Illinois to break off their
affiliation with their motherhouse in Europe: when
the superior refused, he declared the community dismissed
from the diocese, commanded that the Blessed Sacrament
be removed from the convent chapel at Springfield,
and ordered the sisters to leave the city.[27] The sisters
appealed for help to Monsignor Henry Muehlsiepen,
the vicar general of St. Louis. He arranged for them
to stay with the St. Louis Ursulines, but after a while,
he too encouraged them to split from their superiors
in Rome. One group of Precious Blood sisters returned
to Bishop Baltes' jurisdiction, and another stayed in
Bishop Kenrick's diocese. An unusual thing about these
two groups is the charity with which they continued
to regard each other after the split; in many cases,
convent historians describe nuns who left to establish
new communities in terms which would be more appropri-
ate for criminals.

The communities were growing: the new image
of nuns which had emerged from the Oxford movement
and the Civil War made religious life seem more attractive to American girls. The middle class was expanding;
more girls' schools opened to serve this group, and graduates of these schools entered their teachers' communities.
Immigrants from Catholic countries were pouring in.
Girls who could never have become nuns in old Europe
entered American communities where dowries were
not required.

Many new devotional practices were introduced
at this time as parish missions, various confraternities,
and private revelations became popular.

Archbishop Kenrick of St. Louis, an Irishman,
had the German Henry Muehlsiepen as his vicar general;

most dioceses had two men in charge, one to rule the Irish immigrants, and one for the Germans. German immigrants wanted their children taught in German by German nuns in German schools. In some places, St. Louis, for instance, this would continue until 1914. In the 1880s, as other national groups began to settle in American cities, parish priests who were unable to find just what they wanted among the old orders of nuns, formed new congregations to serve in their schools: Polish, Bohemian, Italian.

In the 1890s, the German question caused difficulties inside the communities as the boy question had done in the 1840s. The German schedules, methods of instruction, and traditional devotions were considered oppressive by the young American members of the communities. They wanted to speak and teach and pray in English.

A typical teaching sister of the 1890s got up at three or four, depending upon whether or not it was laundry day. Her room and the convent were cold: nuns sometimes lived in church basements. She would wash, dress, say her prayers, attend Mass, eat breakfast, and then ride an unheated horsecar for one or two hours depending upon how far the parochial school where she taught was from the convent where she lived. She would then begin her teaching day. There would be one hundred or more students in the rows of double desks, rough and hungry immigrant children lucky to be in school instead of at work.[29] At the end of the day, the sister would return home on the horsecars, eat supper, pray, grade papers, fall into bed. In the summer she would return to her motherhouse. The home community would rent extra beds for the sisters coming in from the missions. Like everyone else in nineteenth-century America, nuns slept two or three to a bed; infection spread quickly. The convent graveyards tell the story.[30] Saint Thérèse of the Lisieux Carmel was one of hundreds of young nuns in Europe and America who died of tuberculosis in this period.

Smallpox was another problem. Nuns stopped wearing face veils at this time because people thought they were hiding contagion.[31] Between the Civil War and World War I, most nuns stopped wearing trains;

between World War I and World War II, choir mantels
would disappear.

Communities split over the German question.
Ursulines from Louisville who were teaching in St. Louis
broke from their motherhouse to form an English-speaking
community. The new group was led by a charismatic
musician, Sister Jerome Schaub. The hard feelings caused
by the break are dealt with at length in the communities'
histories: "Father B.H. Westerman, the community's
spiritual director and superior, stood in the way of a
peaceful settlement."[32] The dissenting band had been
emboldened to make the break by a telegram from
Archbishop Kenrick of St. Louis. When the sisters called
on him, they were prevented from seeing him by the
German vicar general, Henry Meuhlsiepen, a friend
of a congregation of German-speaking Ursulines. Kenrick
had never been himself after losing the battle against
papal infallibility: by this time he was incapacitated.
The nuns were rescued by Bishop Fink of Kansas Territory.

The nursing nuns of the 1890s tarnished the reputation for excellence won by the previous generation
in Civil War field hospitals. The nuns' squeamishness
about the human body made them neglect the studies
that would have enabled them to maintain earlier standards.

In spite of the difficulties of the period, many
nuns told convent historians that the 1890s were the
happy days; there was someone to love and to work
for—sometimes a charismatic superior they had risked
everything to follow. There was work to be done, and
each individual sister was important. The new communities lived on rabbits or bread and molasses, and they
sat on packing crates. St. Joseph appeared to them
in various disguises to build a staircase, or prevent
a boiler from exploding, or pay the mortgage. They
worked together, and laughed at their difficulties. They
were freed from some of the old, constricting regulations.
Some were allowed to reach their heights. They had
the satisfaction of building something from nothing,
and seeing it survive. Nuns died on the up-river trips,
and lie buried beside the Missouri. Many young nuns
died of disease, and novices made vows on their
deathbeds. But postulants came to the new communities,

and boarders came to the academies, and the nuns survived.

In 1903 Sister Mary Walsh, founder of the Dominican Sisters of the Sick Poor, told the priest who ruled her community that the newly appointed superior was a drug addict. He refused to believe her, and forced her to go to a rest home for a year without telling anyone the reason. Sister Mary Walsh was vindicated in 1907 when the new superior was dismissed from the community, and hospitalized for drug addiction.[33]

An election held by the Ursuline sisters of Paola, Kansas in 1902, was still tied after three ballots. The rule required that the older in religion be named superior, but Bishop Fink "hammered the table and shook his fist at Sister Leonard. 'You, you cannot be superior. You are not an American citizen. Mother Jerome must be the superior. I will settle the tie. Mother Jerome is superior.' The chapter broke up in confusion. The whole group came from the chapter room in tears..."[34] The new community split apart as a result of the bishop's action.

Mother Walsh of the Dominicans was removed from office by a "plain-spoken monsignor, [who] without first discussing the matter with her, had stated before the assembled sisters that he thought she was too old and nervous to carry all of her former responsibilities."[35]

Mother Walsh once invited benefactors to tea. The priest who directed the community came early. "With the simple pleasure of a child displaying her treasures, she led him to the chapel and showed him the little altar and the statues for which she had paid with the patient work of her hands. 'What wretched taste!' he said coldly, looking about. 'We can't let people see these things.' Curtly he ordered the tea canceled and the invitations withdrawn."[36]

By 1900, the power of bishops and priests over nuns had become absolute. Elections had no force. A superior could be sent away if she failed to agree with a priest. Women considering entering the convent talked to priests who directed them to one community or another; without priests sending new members, communities could not survive. Inhuman treatment of nuns was institutionalized. Nuns learned to express synthetic

feelings and suppress authentic feelings. It was a time
"when nuns were considered only cogs in an educational
system...when the pastor was the undisputed authority."[37]

In the 1913 edition of **Religious Orders of Women
in the United States,** young nuns in beautiful habits
look happy, dignified, and strong. The buildings, the
motherhouses and academies and mission convents,
are substantial and attractive. It is obvious that the
days of penury were over, but problems remained. Nuns
were still overworked and undereducated. Some still
rose for midnight prayer. Several still had lay sisters.[38]

In 1930, a new edition of the book shows the colleges
built by nuns: this was the golden age of Catholic women's
colleges. The nuns chosen to represent their communities
in this edition are older.[39] The founders were dead
or old; the communities now were directed by bureau-
cracies. Individuals were not as important as they had
been in early days; the singular was not tolerated.

Victimhood was the popular devotion in the 1930s,
and the emphasis on silence and penitential practices
increased. The I.H.M. sisters of Michigan were accus-
tomed to "mingling wormwood with their food at table."[40]

"In the Dominican order, whenever a public correction is made by the superior, the offending religious
is required publicly to ask pardon...lying on the floor
on the right side until the correction is made or the
signal is given to rise. This act of reparation is called
the 'venia.'"[41]

In the 1930s the liturgical movement began making
the old prayers seem dated. "If a religious prefers her
private devotions—no matter how legitimate in themselves—to the church's official liturgy, she has not yet
fully entered in to the mind of Christ...."[42] Once again
the prayer life in the communities was changed. In
some convents the Divine Office was reintroduced,
but most nuns continued to say the Little Office and
various devotional prayers. Penitential practices increased. The message given sisters was that they were
sinners, and not to be trusted. The danger nuns faced
from each other was emphasized to an extreme. Friendship, other than in ritual settings, was forbidden.

In a 1944 issue of Sponsa Regis, a priest wrote
about the dangers women faced from other members

of their communities. "At the miasmic breath of particular friendships, the fair and lovely garden of religious
community life withers into a sere and blackened waste.
A particular friendship is something that cannot be
concealed in the community; sometimes it is betrayed
even to outsiders to the scandal of all concerned. I
remember being told how quite a number of years ago
a group of novices visited a community of teaching
sisters. One of the sisters took the novices through
the school and convent. She paused at one room to
speak at length about the young sister who taught there;
she went into detail on the virtues, ability, etc., etc.,
of the sister concerned. Later she brought this sister
down to introduce her to the visitors, and as she made
the introduction, stood with one hand resting on her
friend's arm. The visitors were just innocent novices,
who aren't supposed to notice things, but all of them
noticed that!"[43]

A new catalog of women's communities appeared
in 1955. The requirements for admission to the communities are given, and nuns model the various habits, some
slightly simplified by this time."[44] "I thought I'd gotten
used to being endlessly sticky and smelly, but disgust
with my body became steadily more acute...my underwear
remained black, and it would be days before I was allowed
to change it."[45]

There was talk of sister formation in the 1950s,
and certain nuns began traveling to seminars on the
subject and writing books and articles on the importance
of education for sisters: in spite of the talk, most sisters
still went from the novitiate to parochial school classrooms. They attended college in summer sessions. For
many, summer school was the only vacation they got.
Powerful local superiors ran the missions, and in large
communities, major superiors might know nothing of
an individual sister other than what they learned from
local superiors.

It is said that communities get the superiors they
deserve. Some were lucky, and elected talented, saintly,
loving superiors. Their histories tell of happy days:
"All the sisters who knew her can remember feast days
when, with Mother playing the piano, they sang away
the afternoon."[46] Some communities were less fortunate,

and elected rigid, fearful superiors who added new problems to those inherited from the past.

In the late 1950s, the large generation born in the 1940s, the first generation of Catholics to take secondary education for granted, began entering convents. Their reasons were varied. Some wished to imitate the intellectual and charismatic women who had been their teachers. Some were escaping unhappy home lives, or looking for further education, or hoping for a life more adventurous than that lived by their mothers. Many were disillusioned by what they found in the novitiates. In the Immaculate Heart community of Los Angeles, young women had their heads shaved without previous warning on their first day as novices. They were then introduced to the flagellant devices. "The discipline was a twelve-inch whip, the shaft made of braided venetian blind cord that flowered at the tip into four knotted strips. We were told to use it in private only on Wednesday and Friday afternoons for a specified period of time according to the written regulations, and to use it only on the back, legs, or buttocks. We were never to draw blood...some professed sisters had special permission to wear spiked metal arm bands designed so that the spikes would press into one's flesh on abrupt movement... hair shirts were another form of penance worn by the professed...in their rightful context, they served a serious purpose and seemed no more horrifying than, say, a circumcision rite for teen-age girls as practiced in the prescribed customs of certain primitive tribes."[47]

In an issue of Sponsa Regis from the 1950s, a price list of penitential devices is given. "Full size regular hair shirt: $13.50; hair shirt, large size: $4.50; hair shirt, medium size: $4.00; hair shirt, small size: $3.50; hair cincture: $1.50; hemp discipline, heavy: $1.50; hemp discipline, lighter: $1.00; metal discipline: $1.10; chain cincture: $2.00; chain armlet: 75 cents; leg chain: $1.00. The hair shirts, for your information, are made of sterilized, chemically cleaned horse hair; the hemp disciplines are made of imported Italian flax; and the best quality of stainless steel wire is used for the chains."[48]

A sister told her superior she couldn't take the discipline again: "To me it seems that flagellation is

a means—a perverted means—of sexual satisfaction."
The superior said, "I don't—you don't—none of us knows
what we think until the general chapter tells us."[49]

For those who could not bear the life, there was
no charity. Vocation brochures in the 1950s assured
candidates that it was no disgrace to leave the convent,
but the communities had rules forbidding further contact
with sisters who left. Those who left did so without
saying goodbye. Later, the sisters would be told someone
had gone. They would not speak of her openly again.

The feelings of a friend left behind are expressed
in a poem, "The Departure," by Sister Mary
Jeremy, O.P., of which the following is the first stanza:

What you took with you no one knew.
The night was cold for setting forth;
The wet leaves stirred without a sound
Till the wind wheeled and galloped north.
We listened, but the rain came on
And no one knew when you had gone.[50]

By the end of the 1950s, the novitiates were filled
to overflowing, and communities began planning for
the further education of their new members: many
built juniorates, but most young sisters still went out
to teach without education or credentials. Nuns disappeared in large communities, and realized that they
had vowed to spend their lives being moved from place
to place at the will of others.

In the 1960s religious communities began to call
on psychologists to screen candidates and to counsel
troubled sisters. Many sisters were sent to psychologists
when they told their superiors they wanted to leave.
Some former sisters told of feeling torn by this. Was
wanting to leave religious life a sign of mental instability?
If a nun was sent to a psychiatrist by her superior, was
she under obedience? Was she required to answer a
strange man's questions with absolute candor, even
when they touched areas that she was forbidden to
discuss with other sisters? Was she required to act on
the psychiatrist's suggestions? What if those suggestions
were in opposition to the community's rules? What if
they were repugnant to the sister herself? Many of

the nuns of the present time say that better psychological screening of candidates could have prevented the mass exodus from their orders.

The influx of postulants continued in the early 1960s. Then, in the spring of 1963, at the N.C.E.A. convention in St. Louis, the news about a book spread: **The Nun in the World** brought into focus questions the Vatican Council had suggested. Nuns had begun to examine their lives, and now they split into factions over the difficult questions. What was the reason for wearing costumes designed by nineteenth-century priests? Why did communities hide their histories and the facts of mission life from their youngest members? Why was the history of the church itself presented in such a distorted fashion? What about food? What was the reason for sitting next to the same sister at table for a lifetime? Why were meals eaten in silence? Why were meals with parents forbidden? Why was food not to be enjoyed? Why were novices kept apart from the communities? Why should a grown woman subject another to a public tongue-lashing? What was the purpose of the chapter of faults? What about friends? Why were friends suspected of homosexuality? How could a woman spend a lifetime without friends? "Dying, a sister I had deeply admired admitted to me, 'I have denied myself all human warmth and affection. And now it is too late.'"[51] What about priests? If a priest came into a classroom, the teaching sister was to drop whatever she was doing, and turn her class over to him. If he came to the convent bearing ice cream, the nuns were expected to gush over the childish gift.[52] Priests played with money, withholding sisters' pay checks, and hiding school funds in various accounts.[53] Priests made clumsy sexual advances. "Rigid with disgust, I turned away, trembling, trying not to see his clammy forehead, not to feel the fumbling hands, not to smell the stale egg on his breath...his old body, hands freckled like toads."[54] Nuns were expected to confide in priests who were less educated than they, less sensitive, and openly contemptuous of women. What about education? How could a woman be intellectually honest, a scholar, a teacher, and live in a group where she was not trusted or regarded as an adult? "Jane Austen, Keats, Wordsworth, George Eliot. I felt

like a starving person, about to sample a banquet. Struggling hard, I tried to still my joy. I shouldn't take pleasure
in this. I recalled Mother Walter's strictures about
intellectual pride."[55]

For many religious, the questions had no answers,
and they left. The number of nuns in American convents
peaked at over 181,000 in 1966. After that, the exodus
began. It was the time of the habit question, the Third
Way, the march on Selma, the peace movement, the
English office, the inner city, sunbathing on the roof
of Rogers Hall, guitar Masses, I and Thou, and endless
arguments. The rules directed every moment, waking
and sleeping, and every thought; for one-third of all
nuns, the life had become unendurable. "We lived too
close, but a normal expression of human warmth was
regulated by rule. We did not compliment each other.
We took no time to enjoy the results of a job well done,
for that was a sign of pride. Deprived as we were of
ordinary relaxation, there were under such circumstances
a number of nervous disorders in the community. Guilt
was a constant fact."[56]

Things began to fall apart on a large scale. Cardinal
McIntyre's persecution of the Immaculate Heart community caused it to split apart. A priest, sent by the
cardinal to examine the nuns, asked if there were any
books by non-Catholic authors in the college library.[57]
The high school principals were told to take **Time** magazine out of the libraries because it had run an article
unfavorable to the cardinal. No nun objected.[58] In 1967
the Glenmary order split apart. Fifty members announced
they would live together as lay women. They were unable
to do their apostolic work under the restrictions of
religious life: the archbishop of Cincinnati had given
them new directives about hours, table reading, educational courses, and contacts with laymen.

"The horror of religious life was not, I realized
sadly, what its detractors writing in the tradition of
Maria Monk or the Devils of Loudon, took to be the
dark underside of the convent. It was the emptiness,
the hollowness of a life devoid of human love—however
dedicated to God."[59] Nuns were forbidden the practice
of woman's greatest and first art: conversation. Our
foremothers talked while they worked. Gathering and

talking—the two words come from the same proto-Indo-European root. The gathering women worked with roots, the roots of words and of plants: they learned to select out lovingly just the ones they wanted. The plants became agriculture; the words became literature. Men, hunters whose work required silence and devotion to a leader, came to degrade the women's art. They preferred their rituals, and imposed them on women. Nuns were told that God liked the sound of them all singing and praying together, but disliked the sounds of conversation: ritual was to be preferred to reality. Many former religious mention the sense of unreality they felt in the convent, and many speak of the pain of having no one to talk to. Nuns had to face the terrible possibility of going through life without ever having another honest conversation. They slept where they worked. The boss was always there. The pressure never stopped. There was never time to sit back and relax, and discuss truthfully and with humor or anger or understanding the day's events. It was like being in a never-ending play.

Nuns were forbidden to form friendships. The term "particular friendship" carried the implication of lesbianism. It was not possible for sisters to talk freely with superiors; if the superior spoke with the voice of God, there was no room for give and take. If a sister had a problem, she was usually told to talk to a priest. The contempt many priests felt for nuns was well known. In an article in the January, 1979 issue of **Sisters Today,** Father Roger Kasprick, O.S.B., who edited the magazine from 1963 through 1975, described his feelings about nuns for Sister Mary Anthony, O.S.B., the current editor. "I had sisters in class and associated with them for coffee or lunch. I also had a sort of residual respect and love for sisters. This was undoubtedly because I had never gone to a Catholic grade or high school, so I had never gotten those prejudices against sisters that some priests seemed to have in earlier days."[60]

A former nun: "Why did I leave religious life? Mainly because I had come to realize that I had grown into quite another person from the twenty-two-year-old girl who once felt compelled to 'follow a vocation' and dedicate myself to Catholic education. Today I am convinced that God has really no plan for me other than the one I evolve for myself."[61]

Many women left their communities with no thanks for services rendered, no money for a fresh start, and no explanation of why their gifts had been wasted. Canon law required that communities "in charity"—not in justice—provide for their departing members, but many did not.[62] Many women who left were disoriented about who they were. They were clumsy and afraid. Many believed that leaving the convent meant they were turning their backs on God. The training in submissiveness caused problems with men. Money was a problem for ex-nuns, as was the sudden loss of status. To what social class did an ex-nun belong: her parents' or her old community's? There were illnesses, abortions, debts, suicide attempts, exploitation by men and bosses. For some ex-nuns there were years of wandering. In spite of the difficulties, many former sisters say they would not have missed those years; there was something precious and unforgettable about life in a community of women.

In the 1970s, the communities began to change. The remaining nuns, older and wiser, came to realize that some particular friendships had been like marriages, giving the partners stability and humanity. In some communities, new histories were written to replace earlier unscholarly accounts. Many communities are attempting to return to their original purposes. Nuns are working at jobs they choose, and praying with words of their own. Many religious women are feminists, doing what they can to rid their lives of male dominance and rituals. Small groups of sisters experimented with living apart from the larger communities. Some nuns chose to live alone or with one other sister. The exodus continued. The habits disappeared, and more humane schedules were adapted. Cardinal Suenens' proposals never were implemented. The idea that nuns should exercise a direct apostolate was too surprising and too untraditional. The factions that formed in convents after **The Nun in the World** came out debated the question, but the Catholic culture was unprepared for women pursuing an active, spoken, doctrinal apostolate. The seeking of contact with women and girls for private conversations never began.[63]

In the 1980s, the church is reasserting its power over American nuns. Women are being removed from teaching posts in seminaries. Those who hoped to be ordained are being assured that it will not happen. The Vatican is about to put nuns back into habits. Hospital sisters such as the Sisters of Mercy of the Union are being ordered to bring their practices in line with the pope's views about sterilization. A Vatican official gave a Sister of Mercy of Detroit twenty four hours to give up her job directing a social agency for the state of Michigan: she refused, and was forced to leave her community. An American bishop, Joseph Gossman of Raleigh, North Carolina, attempted in 1983 to speak to the pope on behalf of American sisters. He said he fears "a segment of the church would push women religious back into roles and attitudes of another time."[64] The push continues, and the pope has made it clear that nuns worldwide and American sisters in particular must return to the old ways or leave. The communities have been ordered to write new constitutions and submit them to Rome for approval. The priests who decide how nuns should live send back the constitutions with demands for changes. The changes may be inconsistent and inappropriate, but the sisters must submit or leave.

The pope has ordered American superiors to expel from their communities sisters who signed an advertisement which said a difference of opinion about abortion exists among Catholics. The sisters must recant or leave.

The pope has taken control of the world's 13,000 Carmelite nuns. All must return to a rule written in 1581 by priests. Only a fifth of the nuns, a conservative minority in Spain, desires this life, but all must conform or leave.

Religious communities expel their members without hesitation. The lack of regard for individuals, the fear of friendship, and the tradition of informing on each other make fiction of the idea that the members of a sisterhood comprise a family. The American sisters are old now. They will not find the strength to withstand the new demands from Rome. Instead of being thanked for a lifetime of service, they are being reminded that their assets belong to the Church. If communities of

nuns should be "seduced by the rhetoric that often includes references to a male-dominated Church," and
elect to give up their canonical status, they will lose
everything: buildings they built, academies they toiled
in without rest, the graveyards where their sisters lie;
canon law "would certainly be upheld by the civil
courts."[65] Instead of being left to a peaceful retirement,
sisters are being threatened with financial ruin. They
must return to forms many found alienating, inhuman,
and intolerable—return, or leave.

Notes

1 Charles Currier, **Carmel in America** (Baltimore: John Murphy, 1890).

2 George Parsons Lathrop and Rose Hawthorn Lathrop, **A Story of Courage** (Boston: Houghton, Mifflin, 1894).

3 Henry Churchill Semple, **The Ursulines of New Orleans** (New York: Kenedy, 1925).

4 Lathrop and Lathrop, p. 172.

5 Anna Catherine Minogue, **Loretto, Annals of the Century** (New York: American Press, 1912).

6 Columbia Fox, **Life of John David** (New York: United States Catholic Historical Society, 1925).

7 Katherine Burton, **Make the Way Known** (New York: Farrar, Straus and Cudahy, 1959).

8 There was a tradition dating back to the consecrated virgins of the mystery cults of the ancient world in which escaped nun stories fit nicely. The appetite for prurient material about nuns was at a new height at this time. Not since Boccaccio had so much attention been paid religious women.

9 Sister Mary Faith Schuster, O.S.B., **The Meaning of the Mountain** (Baltimore: Helicon, 1963), pp. 21-22.

10 Mary Jane Coogan, B.V.M., **The Price of Our Heritage** (Dubuque: Mount Carmel Press, 1975).

11 Coogan, p. 323.

12 Coogan, p. 407.

13 Sister Mary George Baska, O.S.B., **The Benedictine Congregation of Saint Scholastica** (Washington, D.C.: Catholic University, 1935).

14 Ray Allen Billington, **The Protestant Crusade** (New York: Rinehart and Company, 1938).

15 Maria Monk, **Awful Disclosures of the Hotel Dieu Nunnery of Montreal** (New York: Howe and Bates, 1836).

16 Mary Ewens, **The Role of the Nun in Nineteenth Century America** (New York: Arno Press, 1978), pp. 130-131.

17 Sister Mary Rosalita, I.H.M., **Achievement of a Century** (Monroe, Michigan: Sisters, Servants of the I.H.M., 1948), pp. 113, 210, 140.

18 Sister Julia Gilmore, **We Came North** (Leavenworth, Kansas: Sisters of Charity, 1958).

19 Ewens, p. 119.

20 Baska, p. 45.

21 Lathrop and Lathrop, p. 123.

22 Ewens, p. 133.

23 Sister Mary Eunice Hanousek, O.S.F., **A New Assisi** (Milwaukee: Bruce, 1948), p. 50.

24 Ellen Ryan Jolly, **Nuns of the Battlefield** (Providence: Visitor Press, 1930), p. 281.

25 **A Story of Fifty Years** (Notre Dame, Indiana: Ave Maria Press, 1902), p. 234.

26 Nuns became standard subjects in murals depicting Civil War scenes and in the poetry of the post-war period. The Jesuits, Abram Ryan and Gerard Manley Hopkins, were among the popular poets who promoted a romantic view of nuns at this time.

27 Member of the Province, **Congregation of the Sisters Adorers of the Most Precious Blood** (Techny, Illinois: Mission Press, 1938), p. 37.

28 Member of the Province, pp. 43-45.

29 Sister Mary Charles McGrath, O.S.U., **Yes Heard Round the World** (Paola, Kansas: Ursuline Sisters, 1978), p. 104. In 1894 a nun wrote from St. Louis to her superior about the 129 pupils in her class. "Father Butler visited the class this morning. When I told him the large number, he replied, 'Oh, there is plenty room for twenty more.'"

30 Schuster, pp. 91-92.

31 Schuster, p. 100.

32 McGrath, p. 78.

33 Anne Cawley Boardman, **Such Love Is Seldom** (New York: Harper Brothers, 1950), pp. 88, 89, 110.

34 McGrath, pp. 127-128.

35 Boardman, p. 181.

36 Boardman, pp. 198-199.

37 McGrath, p. 121.

38 Elinor Tong Dehey, **Religious Orders of Women in the United States** (Hammond, Indiana: Conkey, 1913).

39 Elinor Tong Dehey, **Religious Orders of Women in the United States**, second edition (Hammond, Indiana: Conkey, 1930).

40 Rosalita, p. 115.

41 Boardman, p. 161.

42 Joseph Kreuter, O.S.B., "The Liturgical Movement in Convents," **Sponsa Regis,** September, 1933, reprinted by Daniel Durken, O.S.B. in **Blow the Trumpet at the New Moon** (Collegeville, Minnesota: Liturgical Press, 1979), p. 111.

43 C.O., "Religious Friendship," **Sponsa Regis,** April, 1944, reprinted by Durken, p. 199.

44 **Guide to Catholic Sisterhoods in the United States** (Washington, D.C.: Catholic University, 1955).

45 Karen Armstrong, **Through the Narrow Gate** (New York: St. Martin's Press, 1981), p. 187.

46 McGrath, p. 161. See also Schuster on Mother Lucy Dooley and Sister Helen Louise on **Sister Julia** (New York: Benziger Brothers, 1928).

47 Midge Turk, **The Buried Life** (New York: World Publishing Company, 1971), p. 152.

48 Winfred Herbst, S.D.S., "Convent Queries," **Sponsa Regis,** 1952–1959, reprinted by Durken, pp. 173-4.

49 Armstrong, p. 238.

50 Sister Mary Jeremy, O.P., "The Departure," in **Prose and Poetry of America** (Chicago: L.W. Singer Co., 1940), p. 515.

51 Mary Griffin, **The Courage to Choose** (Boston: Little, Brown, 1975), p. 155.

52 Griffin, p. 158.

53 Turk, p. 127.

54 Armstrong, p. 229.

55 Armstrong, p. 187.

56 Turk, p. 152.

57 Turk, p. 156.

58 Turk, p. 157.

59 Griffin, p. 155.

60 Sister Mary Anthony, O.S.B., "Old Editors Just Fade Away...," **Sisters Today,** January, 1979, reprinted by Durken, p. 29.

61 Griffin, p. 200.

62 Fintan Geser, O.S.B., **The Canon Law Governing Communities of Sisters** (St. Louis: Herder, 1950), p. 349.

63 Joseph Suenens, **The Nun in the World** (Westminster: Newman Press, 1962).

64 "News of the Church," **National Catholic Reporter,** November 11, 1983, p. 3.

65 Richard A. Hill, S.J., "Is Opting Out a No-Win Situation," **National Catholic Reporter,** March 2, 1984, p. 12.

Bibliography

Alma, Sister Maria, C.I.M. **Sisters, Servants of the I.H.M.** Philadelphia: Dolphin Press, 1934.

Armstrong, Karen. **Beginning the World.** New York: St. Martin's Press, 1983.

_____. **Through the Narrow Gate.** New York: St. Martin's Press, 1981.

Barton, George. **Angels of the Battlefield.** Philadelphia: Catholic Art, 1897.

Baska, Sister Mary George, O.S.B. **The Benedictine Congregation of Saint Scholastica,** Washington, D.C.: Catholic University, 1935.

Bernard, Sister Mary. **The Story of the Sisters of Mercy in Mississippi.** New York: Kenedy, 1931.

Billington, Ray Allen. **The Protestant Crusade.** New York: Rinehart and Company, 1938.

Boardman, Anne Cawley. **Such Love Is Seldom.** New York: Harper Brothers, 1950.

Bunkley, Josephine. **The Escaped Nun.** New York: Dewitt and Davenport, 1855.

Burton, Katherine. **Make the Way Known.** New York: Farrar, Straus and Cudahy, 1959.

117

Carroll, Mary Theresa. **Leaves from the Annals of the Sisters of Mercy.** New York: Catholic Publishing Society, 1881.

Charitas, Sister Mary, I.H.M. **Pastoral in Blue.** New York: Scapular Press, 1946.

Clarissa, Mother Mary, and Sister Mary Olivia. **With the Poverello.** New York: P.J. Kenedy and Sons, 1947.

Conyngham, David. **Lives of the Irish Saints.** New York: Sadlier, 1870.

Coogan, Mary Jane, B.V.M. **The Price of Our Heritage.** Dubuque: Mount Carmel Press, 1975.

Currier, Charles. **Carmel in America.** Baltimore: John Murphy, 1890.

Dehey, Elinor Tong. **Religious Orders of Women in the United States.** Hammond, Indiana: Conkey, 1913.

_____. **Religious Orders of Women in the United States,** second edition. Hammond, Indiana: Conkey, 1930.

Doerr, Marie. **Manual for Sister-Visitors.** St. Louis: Catholic Hospital Association, 1967.

Dougherty, Dolorita. **The Sisters of St. Joseph of Carondolet.** St. Louis: Herder, 1966.

Downing, Margaret. **Chronicles of Loretto.** New York: McBride, 1897.

Durken, Daniel, O.S.B., Editor. **Blow the Trumpet at the New Moon.** Collegeville, Minnesota: The Liturgical Press, 1979.

Eckenstein, Lina. **Women Under Monasticism.** New York: Russell and Russell, 1963.

Ellis, John Tracy, and Robert Trasco. **A Guide to American Catholic History.** Santa Barbara, California: ABC Clio, 1982.

Eleanore, Sister Mary. **On the King's Highway.** New York: Appleton, 1931.

Eulalia Teresa, Sister Mary, S.N.J.M. **So Short a Day.** New York: McMullen Books, 1954.

Ewens, Mary. **The Role of the Nun in Nineteenth-Century America.** New York: Arno Press, 1978.

Fecher, Con. **Life-Style and Demography of Catholic Religious Sisterhoods.** Dayton: University of Dayton Press, 1975.

Fitzgerald, Sister Mary Paul, S.C.L. **Beacon on the Plains.** Leavenworth, Kansas: St. Mary's College, 1939.

Fox, Columbia. **Life of John David.** New York: United States Catholic Historical Society, 1925.

Gately, Sister Mary Josephine. **The Sisters of Mercy.** New York: Macmillan, 1931.

Geser, Fintan, O.S.B. **The Canon Law Governing Communities of Sisters.** St. Louis: Herder, 1950.

Gilmore, Sister Julia, S.C.L. **We Came North.** Leavenworth, Kansas: Sisters of Charity, 1958.

Goerres, Ida. **The Hidden Face.** New York: Pantheon. 1959.

Goffman, Irving. **Asylums.** New York: Doubleday, 1982.

Gohmann, Sister Mary de Lourdes, O.S.U. **Chosen Arrows.** New York: Pageant Press, 1957.

Griffin, Mary. **The Courage to Choose.** Boston: Little, Brown, 1975.

Guide to the Catholic Sisterhoods in the United States. Washington, D.C.: Catholic University, 1955.

Hanousek, Sister Mary Eunice, O.S.F. **A New Assisi.** Milwaukee: Bruce, 1948.

Hassard, John. **The Life of John Hughes.** New York: Arno Press, 1969.

Hayes, James M. **The Bon Secours Sisters in the United States.** Washington, D.C.: 1931.

Helen Louise, Sister. **Sister Julia.** New York: Benziger Brothers, 1928.

Holland, Sister Mary Ildephonse, R.S.M. **Lengthened Shadows.** New York: Bookman, 1952.

Hrdy, Sarah Blaffer. **The Woman That Never Evolved.** Cambridge, Massachusetts: Harvard University Press, 1981.

Hurley, Sister Helen Angela. **On Good Ground.** Minneapolis: University Press, 1981.

Images of Women in Mission. Ramsey, New Jersey: Paulist Press, 1981.

In the Early Days. Dubuque, Iowa: St. Joseph's Convent, 1911.

Jameson, Anna. **Sisters of Charity, Catholic and Protestant.** Boston: Ticknor and Fields, 1857.

Jean Patricia, Sister Mary. **Only One Heart.** New York: Doubleday, 1963.

Jolly, Ellen Ryan. **Nuns of the Battlefield.** Providence, Rhode Island: Providence Visitor Press, 1930.

Kane, George. **Twice Called.** Milwaukee: Bruce, 1959.

Kopp, Sister Lilanna. **Sudden Spring.** Culver City, California: Sisters for Christian Community, 1980.

Lanslots, D.I., O.S.B. **Handbook of Canon Law for Congregations of Women Under Simple Vows.** New York: Pustet, 1909.

Lathrop, George Parsons, and Rose Hawthorn Lathrop. **A Story of Courage.** Boston: Houghton, Mifflin, 1894.

Lennon, Sister Mary Isidore, R.S.M. **Milestones of Mercy.** Milwaukee: Bruce, 1957.

Lexau, Joan M., Editor. **Convent Life.** New York: Dial Press, 1964.

Loretta, Sister Mary. **Amazonia.** New York: Pageant, 1963.

Ludovicka, Mary. **Our Community.** La Crosse, Wisconsin: St. Rose Convent, 1920.

Lund, Candida, Editor. **Nunsuch: Stories About Sisters.** Chicago: Thomas More Press, 1982.

Ludwig, Sister Mary Mileta, F.S.P.A. **A Chapter of Franciscan History.** New York: Bookman, 1950.

Malard, Suzanne. **Un Million de Religieuses.** Paris: Fayard, 1960.

Mannix, Mary E. **Memoirs of Sister Louise.** Boston: Angel Guardian Press, 1907.

Marie of the Incarnation, O.S.U. **Autobiography.** Chicago: Loyola University Press, 1964.

Martindale, C.C., S.J. **The Foundress of the Sisters of the Assumption.** London: Burns, 1936.

McAllister, Anna Shannon. **Flame in the Wilderness.** Notre Dame, Indiana: Sisters of the Holy Cross, 1944.

McCann, Sister Mary Agnes. **The History of Mother Seton's Daughters.** New York: Longmans, 1917.

McDonald, Sister Mary Grace, O.S.B. **With Lamps Burning.** St. Joseph, Minnesota: St. Benedict's Priory Press, 1957.

McGill, Anna Blanche. **The Sisters of Charity of Nazareth, Kentucky.** New York: Encyclopedia Press, 1917.

McGrath, Sister Mary Charles, O.S.U. **Yes Heard Round the World.** Paola, Kansas: Ursuline Sisters, 1978.

McGreal, Sister Mary Nona, O.P. **The Role of a Teaching Sisterhood in American Education.** Washington, D.C.: Catholic University of America Press, 1951.

Member of the Community. **Our Community.** La Crosse, Wisconsin: St. Rose Convent, 1920.

Member of the Congregation. **A Retrospect: Three Score and Ten.** New York: Benziger Brothers, 1916.

Member of the Province. **Congregation of the Sisters Adorers of the Most Precious Blood: Providence of Ruma.** Techny, Illinois: Mission Press, 1938.

Member of the Scranton Community. **The Sisters of the I.H.M.** New York: Kenedy, 1921.

Meyers, Sister Bertrande, D.C. **Sisters for the 21st Century.** New York: Sheed and Ward, 1965.

Minogue, Anna Catherine. **Loretto, Annals of the Century.** New York: American Press, 1912.

Monk, Maria. **Awful Disclosures of the Hotel Dieu Nunnery of Montreal.** New York: Howe and Bates (Harper Brothers), 1836.

Mug, Sister Mary Theodosia, Editor. **Journals and Letters of Mother Theodore Guerin.** St. Mary of the Woods, Indiana: Providence Press, 1936.

Murphy, Dominick. **Sketches of Irish Nunneries.** Dublin: Duffy, 1865.

O'Gorman, Edith. **Trials and Persecutions.** Hartford: Connecticut Publishing Company, 1871.

Patricia Jean, Sister, S.L. **Only One Heart.** New York: Doubleday, 1963.

Power, Eileen. **Medieval English Nunneries.** Cambridge: Cambridge University Press, 1922.

Reed, Rebecca. **Six Months in a Convent.** New York: Leavitt, Lord, 1835.

Ritamary, Sister, C.H.M., Editor. **Planning for the Formation of Sisters.** New York: Fordham University Press, 1958.

Rosalita, Sister Mary, I.H.M. **Achievement of a Century.** Monroe, Michigan: Sisters, Servants of the I.H.M., 1948.

_____. **No Greater Service.** Detroit: Sisters, Servants of the I.H.M., 1948.

St. George, Mother Mary Edmond, O.S.U. **An Answer to Six Months in a Convent, Exposing the Falsehoods and Manifold Absurdities.** Boston: Eastburn, 1835.

Savage, Sister Mary Lucida, C.S.J. **The Congregation of St. Joseph of Carondolet.** St. Louis: B. Herder, 1923.

Schuster, Sister Mary Faith, O.S.B. **The Meaning of the Mountain.** Baltimore: Helicon, 1963.

Segale, Sister Blandina. **At the End of the Santa Fe Trail.** Milwaukee: Bruce, 1948.

Semple, Henry Churchill. **The Ursulines of New Orleans.** New York: Kenedy, 1925.

Sister of Charity of the B.V.M. **In the Early Days.** St. Louis: Herder, 1912.

Sister of the Holy Cross. **A Story of Fifty Years.** Notre Dame, Indiana: Ave Maria Press, 1912.

Sister of the Precious Blood. **Not with Silver or Gold.** Dayton: Sisters of the Precious Blood, 1945.

Sitwell, Sacheverell. **Monks, Nuns, and Monasteries.** New York: Holt, 1965.

Steele, Francesca M. **The Convents of Great Britain.** St. Louis: Herder, 1902.

A Story of Fifty Years. Notre Dame, Indiana: Ave Maria Press, 1902.

Suenens, Joseph. **The Nun in the World.** Westminster: Newman Press, 1962.

Thomas, Evangeline, C.S.J. **Women Religious History Sources.** New York: R.R. Bowker Company, 1983.

Travelers on the Way of Peace. Yankton, South Dakota: Order of St. Benedict, 1955.

Tumasz, Florence. **They Walked in His Ways.** Philadelphia: Holy Family College, 1979.

Turk, Midge. **A Buried Life.** New York: World, 1971.

Villet, Barbara. **Those Whom God Chooses.** New York: Viking Press, 1966.

Wand, Augustin, S.J., and Sister Mary Lilliana Owens, S.L., Editors. **Documents: Nerinckx—Kentucky— Loretto.** St. Louis: Loretto Library and Benevolent Institution, 1972.

Whelan, Dom Basil, O.S.B. **Historic English Convents of Today.** London: Burns, Oates, & Washbourne, 1936.

Wong, Mary. **Nun, A Memoir.** New York: Harcourt, 1982.

Index